Indian English
Language & Culture

Indian English Language & Culture
1st edition – September 2008

Published by
Lonely Planet Publications Pty Ltd ABN 36 005 607 983
90 Maribyrnong St, Footscray, Victoria 3011, Australia

Lonely Planet Offices
Australia Locked Bag 1, Footscray, Victoria 3011
USA 150 Linden St, Oakland CA 94607
UK 2nd floor, 186 City Road, London, EC1V 2NT

Cover
Indian montage by Yukiyoshi Kamimura
© Lonely Planet Publications Pty Ltd 2008

ISBN 978 1 74059 576 6

text © Lonely Planet Publications Pty Ltd 2008

10 9 8 7 6 5 4 3 2

Printed by The Bookmaker International Ltd, China

ACKNOWLEDGMENTS

Lonely Planet language products would like to acknowledge the following people for their contributions to this book:

Shinie Antony, who considers Indian English the Loch Ness monster of all languages – all have heard about it but none can locate its source. Shinie has been a subeditor with leading financial dailies in India and has written four novels: *Barefoot And Pregnant*, *Planet Polygamous*, *Kardamom Kisses* and *Seance On A Sunday Afternoon*. She won the Asia Award for story writing from the Commonwealth Broadcasting Association in 2002 and is currently based in Bengaluru.

Craig Scutt, who was at an illegal rave in England the first time he heard the word 'pukka' and is convinced that something very tantric and serene moved him to discover the origins of the word while researching this book. He is looking forward to the future when everyone speaks Indian English and he can get a real job as an interpreter.

Rajesh Devraj, who is an expert on all things Indian English and provided great insight and guidance. He is the author of the blog on Indian English *Dick & Garlick* (http://dickandgarlick.blogspot.com/).

Vivek Wagle, a Lonely Planet colleague, who lent us his expertise on Indian sport and literature.

Piers Kelly, who helped out with the early chapters by supplying his linguistic and editorial expertise and expert turn of phrase.

Lonely Planet Language Products

Associate Publisher: Ben Handicott

Commissioning Editor & Project Manager:
Karin Vidstrup Monk

Editor: Robyn Loughnane

Assisting Editors: Laura Crawford & Francesca Coles

Managing Editors: Annelies Mertens & Bruce Evans

Layout Designers: Cara Smith & Pablo Gastar

Managing Layout Designers:
Celia Wood & Adam McCrow

Cartographer: Wayne Murphy

Series Designer, Cover & Illustrations:
Yukiyoshi Kamimura

CONTENTS

India

Afghanistan

Northern Areas

KARAKORAM

China

Srinagar • JAMMU & KASHMIR

HIMACHAL PRADESH

Shimla •

PUNJAB

Chandigarh •

HARYANA

Dehra Dun

UTTARANCHAL

GREAT HIMALAYA RANGE

Tibet

Pakistan

⊙ Delhi

UTTAR PRADESH

Nepal

SIKKIM

Gangtok •

Bhutan

ARUNACHAL PRADE

• Lucknow

Guwahati (Gauhati)

ASSAM

NAGALAND

Great Desert of Thar

• Jaipur

Patna •

BIHAR

MEGHALAYA

MANIPUR

RAJASTHAN

Bangladesh

TRIPURA

JHARKHAND

Gandhinagar •

• Bhopal

• Ranchi

WEST BENGAL

MIZORAM

GUJARAT

MADHYA PRADESH

Kolkata (Calcutta)

Mya (Bu

Raipur •

ORISSA

CHHATTISGARH

• Bhubaneswar

Arabian Sea

Mumbai (Bombay)

MAHARASHTRA

Bay of Bengal

• Hyderabad

ANDHRA PRADESH

Panaji (Panjim) •

GOA

KARNATAKA

Lakshadweep Islands (India)

LAKSHADWEEP

Bengaluru (Bangalore) •

• Chennai (Madras)

Andaman Islands (India)

Andan Sea

ANDAMAN & NICOBAR ISLANDS

KERALA

TAMIL NADU

0 _____ 500 km
0 _____ 250 mi

INDIAN OCEAN

Thiruvananthapuram (Trivandrum) •

Sri Lanka

INDIAN OCEAN

Nicobar Islands (India)

Maldives

■ highland

■ desert

■ seasonal marsh

Central Asia

China

Middle East

INDIA

Southeast Asia

Indian Ocean

Note: The external borders of India have not been authenticated and may not be correct.

COUNTRY MAP

6

Introduction

'Indian English' is the informal way Indians speak English – their colourful Indian-flavoured take on the English language. The interesting tale of Indian English stretches all the way back to 31 December 1600, when Queen Elizabeth I granted a trade monopoly over India to a handful of London businessmen. Her actions paved the way for the British East India Company's foray into India. The result was over 300 years of trade and conflict. One of the most powerful and lasting legacies of British involvement in India, however, is the language that was left behind.

It wasn't until the 1830s that the move towards Indians speaking English began in earnest. The colonial powers decided to educate what would become a privileged class of Indians to serve as a military and administrative barrier between them and the general population. Members of this new elite were schooled in a British-style system, with all lessons taught in English.

In India, English is an official language of government and an important medium of communication for business. By some estimates, India now has more speakers of English than any other country in the world, although these mostly speak English as a second language.

The version of English taught at English medium schools in India was, and in some cases continues to be, British English.

Introduction

WHICH ENGLISH?

If you'd always thought that English is just English and that's that, we've got some news for you – there are actually many distinct varieties of English around the world, which differ in more than just accent. For example, Australian English, Singapore English, Irish English and South African English all have elements of vocabulary and grammar that set them apart from one another, and each is considered a standard variety in its own right. The following is a quick guide to the different varieties of English referred to in this book:

American English is, of course, English as it is spoken in the USA, as opposed to other English-speaking countries. While there are many regional varieties of American English, it is the standard newsreader and Hollywood varieties which currently permeate India.

British English is, simply, English as it is spoken in Britain, encompassing its many regional varieties. The particular kind of British English which has been most influential in India, however, is the posh-sounding, old-school queen's English, once spoken by the educated upper classes of Britain.

Hinglish is an on-the-fly mixture of English and Hindi words in the one sentence. It is different to Indian English in that it is not (or at least not yet) a distinct language or dialect of its own – it can be English with a few Hindi words thrown in, or Hindi with a few English words thrown in. Some more persistent Hinglish inventions have, however, been incorporated into standard Indian English. The same process occurs with the many other languages spoken in India, such as Tamil and Bengali, resulting in Tanglish (Tamil and English) and Benglish (Bengali and English).

Indian English is the modern variety of English spoken in India. It is a full-blown, here-to-stay variety of English, with its own native speakers, grammar and vocabulary. It is similar to, but distinct from, other varieties of English around the world and like many other Englishes, it consists of subvarieties, with differing regional varieties, eg Delhi Indian English, as well as socio-economic varieties, eg educated Indian English.

Received Pronunciation is one of the accents of British English speakers. Although it is the mother-tongue accent of only a small minority, it used to be the accent to which many Britons aspired. Think old-BBC-style newsreader.

Standard English is a kind of average, idealised or standardised English. It is more of a concept than a reality, and can't be pinpointed to a particular variety of English, but it approaches the forms of English spoken by educated people around the world.

This was the form of English spoken during the British Raj and the variety which Indians aspired to speak. It was characterised by a Received Pronunciation accent (see box above) and an adherence to traditional ideas of grammatical correctness, which would sound well beyond excessive to modern-day speakers of English.

Even after India gained independence in 1947, British English continued to be taught as the proper, indeed the only, way to speak English. As late as the 1970s, when British regional accents were starting to make an appearance on British television, Indians were learning their English grammar from textbooks half a century out of date (see box p13). But while British English was being taught in the hallowed classrooms of the country's most prestigious schools, the variety of English spoken in India at large was morphing into something else altogether.

That something else is what this book attempts to describe. Over two turbulent centuries the language of the colonial rulers has been bent to better suit the needs and will of its Indian masters. It has absorbed words and idioms from India's indigenous languages, and some of its grammar has been rewired in the mould of Hindi, Gujarati, Marathi, Urdu and India's hundreds of other languages.

SANSKRIT INFLUENCE

Long before English arrived, Sanskrit was an important language in India and remains so today. The influence of Sanskrit has even trickled through into standard English, with words like *karma* (from the Sanskrit meaning 'action, effect'), *swastika* (from *svastika* 'symbol of good luck'), and *mantra* (literally 'speech') all originating in this ancient tongue.

As the classical language of ancient India, Sanskrit's prestigious status is similar to that of Latin in Europe. Referred to as the 'language of the gods', it emerged as early as 3500 years ago and is, in many ways, the mother of many modern Indian languages. Arguably Sanskrit's biggest claim to fame is as the sacred language of Hinduism, India's main religion. As a result, it has had a strong influence on Hindi and many other languages of India. Ancient scriptures, like the *Veda Grantha*, and epics such as the *Mahabharata* and *Ramayana*, are all written in Sanskrit. The language also plays a key role in Buddhist literature.

Sanskrit no longer has any native speakers but its strong impact on the modern languages of India can still be detected in their vocabulary and grammar.

The beginnings of Indian English

Indian English began to emerge as a separate variety soon after the broader population began taking on English as a preferred second language. But the influences which would later shape Indian English into what it is today were brewing long before the British arrived – languages of other colonial powers, as well as classical Sanskrit (see box below), were already influential in India.

SANSKRIT & BEYOND

Did you know that English and other European languages are distantly related to Sanskrit and many other languages from India? The chart below shows some words in Sanskrit, Latin, German and English which have striking similarities in form, eg all the words for 'month' start with an *m*-sound. This is not a bizarre coincidence – these words are similar because they all purported to come from a single ancestor language that scholars term Proto-Indo-European.

Sanskrit	Latin	German	English
mās	mensis	Monat	month
matar	mater	Mutter	mother
nakt	nox	Nacht	night
nās	nasus	Nase	nose
nava	novux	neu	new
trayas	tres	drei	three

EARLY EUROPEAN INFLUENCE

Long before the British Raj secured its dominance over the subcontinent, European merchants fought to establish a physical, and consequently also linguistic, presence in India. The Portuguese and French were the first travelling traders to really get a foothold in the lucrative exotica of the Indian market, and were later followed by the Dutch, among others.

During the spice trade with India, Europeans imported elements of their respective languages into the country. As a coastal lingua franca, Portuguese was by far the most influential, introducing words such as *pao* 'bread' (from Portuguese *pão*) and *almirah* 'cupboard' (from Portuguese *armário*) into the local languages of India. Conversely, many Indian words in standard English, including 'bamboo' and 'curry', are believed to have been imported from local Indian languages via Portuguese.

BRITISH INFLUENCE

Britain's East India Company first set up shop in Surat in 1610 before shifting base to Calcutta (Kolkata). However, the first formal effort to spread English amongst the broader populace was made by Lord Thomas Babington Macaulay during his tenure as a member of the Supreme Council of India. In the 1830s he set himself the goal of creating 'a class who may be interpreters between us and the millions whom we govern – a class of persons, Indians in blood and colour, but English in taste, in opinion, in morals and in intellect'.

Indians who wanted their children to get ahead in life – that is, get a job working in the colonial administration – had to send them to boarding school where they were taught British English, which they used as their primary means of communication. It is also worthy of note, however, that many prominent educational institutions were also set up by Indians themselves as part of an agenda to educate their own communities. The Hindu College, for example, was the first institution to provide a Western liberal education for its students, and was set up by Indians in 1817, long before the British even had an education policy. Graduates of the Hindu College would later serve in the Raj, alongside those who hailed from schools established by the British.

Through this new Indian elite, British English would supposedly trickle down and be understood by the general population. But while the elite conformed to the rules of speaking British English, less privileged Indians, who picked up English in addition to their mother tongue and other languages, naturally bent the language to a form more suited to their own ears and tongues. And so began the processes of adding words from indigenous languages, of literally translating colloquial Indian phrases into English, and of dropping or adding various sounds and syllables.

At the same time as the British were imposing their language on the Indian population, words were flowing in the opposite direction. The British needed to adapt their language in order to run the colonial administration, which is why indigenous terms like *punkah* (fan), *coolie* (porter), and *lathi* (police cane) entered the British English vocabulary throughout the 19th century.

But to Indians brought up with English as their first language, the idea of blemishing their mother tongue with supposedly barbarian words or turns of phrase was anathema. They began

---

STANDARD TEXT

The ubiquitous textbooks known simply by the authors' names, *Wren and Martin*, were the standard textbooks used in Indian schools to teach English grammar up until recently. This is despite the fact that they were first published in 1935 and were written for the offspring of British officials posted in India. The antiquated books have now become the subject of affectionate nostalgia for many educated Indians.

to look down on their fellow countrymen who could not grasp the grammatical complexities and lordly accent of the queen's English. Even today the snob value in India associated with speaking 'good' English is yet to fully disappear.

Despite its links to the British colonisers, English is now a lingua franca that bridges India's cultural and linguistic divides. For centuries India had no universal tongue, and the fact that people living at different ends of the country spoke (and still speak) different indigenous languages formed a barrier to easy communication. When mutinous *sepoys* (Indian soldiers) of the East India Company took over the telegraph system in 1857, they could not use it to rally support as they had no common language that could link, for example, Kamptee with Kanpur, two of the centres of insurrection. By the time India achieved independence in 1947, however, the usefulness of English as a lingua franca had long been recognised.

DRIVING THE ENGLISH LANGUAGE OUT

In his groundbreaking work, *Hind Swaraj* (Home Rule) from 1910, Mahatma Gandhi argues that Hindi should be India's universal language, written in Persian or Nagari characters. By using both, Hindus and Mohammedans (Muslims) would be brought closer together in order to efficiently drive out the English language.

POST-INDEPENDENCE

On 15 August 1947 the Union Jack was removed from the Lal Qila (Red Fort) in Delhi. Finally, the Raj was over and India was declared *swatantra* (independent). When India's elastic borders snapped shut behind the retreating British army, the government had the chance to raise the question of what would be the national language, a challenge given the linguistic diversity of India: with a population which currently numbers more than a billion people, there are about 30 languages with more than a million native speakers, a further 60 or so with more than 100,000 speakers and more than 100 with more than 10,000 native speakers each. The number of dialects runs into thousands.

The most widely spoken and understood official language in India is currently Hindi, which is largely due to the prominent role the language played in India's precolonial history when India was a collection of principalities.

But, even after Hindi was adopted as the official national language, it failed to unify the country. Hindi is an Indo-Aryan language, which originated in northern India. Indians living elsewhere and speaking a different first language weren't exactly over the moon when they were suddenly expected to learn Hindi. After years of protest and occasional outbursts of violence, the central government allowed each state government to choose its own first language. Hence Bihar in eastern India has two official languages – Hindi and Urdu. In addition to English, there are 22 languages that are officially recognised at both state and central government levels (see chapter 10 for more on the official languages of India). But the only language among them that can truly claim to oil the cogs of business and government alike is English, whether spoken as standard English or Indian English.

Due to its lack of ties to precolonial history, English in any form does not generate the same depth of emotion and suspicion as India's indigenous tongues. Given the somewhat dubious conduct of the British in India, this might seem bizarre. Yet despite occasional calls from nationalists to abandon it, the majority of Indians continue to embrace English.

Indian English in full bloom

If India's old teachers had had it their way, there would be no Indian English. Not only did they expect students to produce grammatically correct English but, until the last quarter of the 20th century, their goal was to get students to speak and write an incredibly formal variety of British English, akin to the queen's English. As the 20th century came to an end, however, it became evident that no-one in the world, not even in Buckingham Palace, was still speaking the kind of idealised British English that India's teachers were aiming for.

During this period, the school system expanded with the aim of providing a universal standard of education for all. The rate of education growth in India has been astounding. State figures show that in 1950–51 only 3.1 million students were enrolled for primary education. By 1997–98 the figure was 39.5 million. But while expensive private schools produce graduates who speak perfect standard English as their teachers envisioned, the majority of schools can only claim partial success.

Along with the expansion of the education system, the fact that employment prospects are linked to good English skills has lead to an explosion of English in India. Local newspapers and websites abound with advertisements for English teachers and institutions offering TOEFL (Test of English as a Foreign Language) courses. With so many people wanting to learn the language, it is possible that previous estimates of 350 million (mostly second-language) English speakers in India might have already been surpassed.

LANGUAGE OF OPPORTUNITY

In India, English is booming in popularity. The number one reason for this is the obvious link between English-language skills and employment. The upwardly mobile have always been inclined to enrol their children in the English-medium schools, and today English, as the language of business, is seen as an investment in a child's future, a security blanket, and mandatory for plum *babu* (bureaucratic) posts in the government.

During a visit to New Delhi in 2008, David L Hunt, vice president of the world's largest private educational testing and measurement service provider, ETS (Educational Testing Service), said 'India is a global economy and people dealing with international clients need to speak better English.' He was referring to staff employed by India's booming call-centre industry. – IANS (Indo-Asian News Service)

It is estimated that there are at least a quarter of a million Indians working in call centres. While conditions in some of these are said to cause stress and high staff turnover, the wages are relatively high, so there is heavy competition for these jobs. Applicants with the best English skills , meaning those who can speak standard English and sound like a native of Britain, America, Australia, or any of the other countries that are outsourcing to call centres in India, usually get the position.

The ability to speak English connotes better education, better prospects and better class, and what was once the 'language of the elite' is now the 'language of opportunity'.

CHUTNEYFICATION

English is very much the word on the street, which is exactly where you'll find it: scrawled across street hoardings, and used in billboard advertising, cinema posters and even food labels. English is the ubiquitous medium of communication in India

Most Indians who speak English, however, do so as a second or third language. And it's the natural influence from their mother tongues which has played a major role in the *chutneyfication* (Indianisation, derived from the name for the beloved Indian condiment) of the English language in India. In choosing which English words to use, Indians consciously or subconsciously seek to retain an Indian flavour. As one of the most multilingual nations on earth, Indian English closes the divide between Indians who speak different first languages.

The mannerisms, idioms and parts of speech found in indigenous tongues have been incorporated into the way English is spoken in India and this, more than anything, is what gives Indian English its unique flavour.

From a historic and cultural perspective, one of the quaintest aspects of Indian English is the number of vestigial words and phrases left over from the earlier forms of British English spoken in India.

Phrases that have been abandoned in English elsewhere in the world are still common in India, especially in the press. Where else could you seriously expect to hear that *miscreants abound* and *dastardly deeds* are done before *sleuths nab the man*? Archaic-sounding terms like *tomfoolery* and *balderdash* are like linguistic time capsules buried within the fabric of Indian English.

On the one hand they represent a colonial hangover, but on the other there's also a great deal of nostalgia at play, which makes it heart-warming to know that across this vast nation the *needful* is still being done, the bereaved are *condoled*, a mistress is a *concubine*, a tough job is a *daunting task*, and *high drama* denotes needless fuss.

HINGLISH

Hinglish is the seemingly random mixing of English with Hindi to form words or sentences that can only be comprehended by speakers fluent in both languages. With over 180 million Indians who regard Hindi as their mother tongue, and around another 120 million who use it as their second language, Hindi has had a strong influence on the way English is spoken in India.

Hinglish has produced some of the most memorable phrases you can expect to hear in India such as *brain fail ho gaya* (brain failed) and *dimag out ho gaya* (brain was out), which both mean 'behaving like an idiot'.

The signs that Hinglish is here to stay are easy to spot. Billboard and TV advertising regularly uses Hinglish to sell products and Bollywood has produced scores of Hinglish movies. The 'coolness' associated with Hinglish was evident in the popularity of Bharat Dabholkar, one of the pioneers of Hinglish in advertising. In his heyday, the ponytailed scriptwriter was part of India's 'it' crowd; he was often seen surrounded by models and kept live piranhas in a special tank in his office.

The following are a few common Hinglish expressions:

bahut bore	very boring (from Hindi *bahut* for 'a lot')
ekdum fit	perfectly suited (from Hindi *ekdum* for 'completely')
ek minute	one minute (from Hindi *ek* for 'one')
fansofied	captured (from Hindi *fansana*, to 'trap')
kya problem hai?	what is the problem? (from Hindi *kya* for 'what')
love mein	in love (from Hindi *mein* for 'in')
maha idiot	mega idiot (from Hindi *maha* for 'very')
police chowki	police station (from Hindi *chowki* for 'platform')

IMPACT ON NATIVE LANGUAGES

There are hundreds of languages and thousands of dialects spoken in India. Ever since English was accepted, along with Hindi, as the joint official language of government and the language of business, there have been fears it would affect the existence of these indigenous regional languages. Until recently such fears seemed ill founded, but times have changed and more and more people are now speaking English or another official language instead of the native languages that their parents and grandparents spoke.

At most government schools, classes are conducted in the main regional language. In Bengaluru (formerly Bangalore), for example, lessons take place in Kannada, the official state language, rather than the smaller indigenous languages. Although this may arrest the decline of Kannada, many also argue that failure to conduct classes in English ruins students' employment prospects in a global marketplace. For better or worse, there is a growing sense that English is the only language you need in order to get ahead. As more young Indians flock to the cities in search of fortune, they are abandoning their native and regional languages in favour of Indian English.

This phenomenon has linguists worried. K. David Harrison, author of *When Languages Die* (2006), paints a gloomy picture:

The pace of language extinction we're seeing, it's really unprecedented in human history. And it's happening faster than the extinction of flora and fauna. More than 40% of the world's languages could be considered endangered compared to 8% of plants and 18% of mammals.

By permission of Oxford University Press

But there is hope: Indians are acutely aware of the value of their languages and the need to preserve them. One Mumbai billboard carried the slogan, 'Choose your language for your power bill', offering people the choice of receiving their bill in either Marathi, Hindi, Gujarati or English.

AMERICAN REVOLUTION

It is likely that, in a matter of only a few years, the voices of even the most ardent advocates of the queen's English will be drowned under a cacophony of American-influenced drawl. Indians could soon be mocking British tourists for the way they pronounce 'tomato'.

While British English continues to hold sway in bureaucratic and academic circles, a new charm offensive has been launched by American English – via Hollywood, TV serials, bestsellers and billboard hits. The newer generation of Indians is attracted to the casual, fun quotient in American English and have already begun to adopt it in speech. Even spellings have begun to tilt towards this trend – perhaps mostly due to the computer spell checkers.

American English is simpler in many cases, replacing 'ou' with 'o' as in 'rumor' and 'labor' and nudging verbs ending with 'ise' to 'ize', and it is increasingly felt that these spellings connect the reader quicker to the writer as it cuts back alphabetical flab. Indians are definitely more aware of American English than ever before and consider it neither superior nor inferior to British English, but a viable alternative to British English in the sphere of speech and spellings.

American English has influenced Indian English by introducing colloquialisms, such as *man*, *dude* and *cool*. Hollywood celebrities are now part of India's staple diet of conversation, whereas the only other foreigners of interest are sports stars such as Australian cricket legend Shane Warne and football's 'golden balls' David Beckham. In the battle for hearts, minds, pronunciation and spelling, American English is winning hands down.

SPEAKING INDIAN ENGLISH

If standard English is bangers and mash, Indian English is mango and chilli. Throughout the subcontinent its trademark fast pace, clipped diction and sing-song lilt bubble up from marketplaces, television sets, bus stops, meeting rooms and cafés. Indians have lost no time in making the imported English language their own, infusing it with a heady blend of indigenous words, colloquialisms and playful idioms. The versatility and diversity of Indian English is truly remarkable – it can be adapted to express a refined formality as much as casual intimacy, enchanting poetry and sheer absurdity. Above all, Indian English is distinctly, well, *Indian*. Spicy, subtle, cheekily quaint and fun.

Indian English is evolving at lightning pace and is greatly influenced by media, music trends and the Indian sense of humour. If a catchy turn of phrase is broadcast on TV one day, you'll be hearing it ad infinitum on the streets the next. Keep up if you can!

It's rare for speakers of other varieties of English to have real difficulty understanding the way Indian English is spoken, but taking the time to understand some of the fundamental elements – pronunciation, grammar, vocabulary and cultural functions – will deepen your appreciation of this fascinating variety.

I think you will be loving Indian English, isn't it?

Pronunciation

The pronunciation of Indian English can vary from region to region within the country. Given the diversity of India's indigenous languages, this is hardly surprising; it's the sounds from a speaker's first language that have the greatest influence on the pronunciation of their second language. The sound patterns from the native tongue – the consonants, vowels, pitch and stress – combine to colour English as it's spoken in India. Southern Indians, for example, curl the tongue more for *l* and *n* sounds, so that the word 'total' comes out sounding more like the American pronunciation of 'turtle'. Bengalis and Biharis substitute a *j* sound in place of a *z* sound so 'zero' ends up sounding like *jero*. Many Indian English speakers change *w* sounds to *v* sounds and vice versa, so in some parts of the country the word 'wine' sounds more like *vine*, in others the word 'vine' will be pronounced *wine*. Meanwhile, the *th* sounds can come out sounding like a *t* or a *d*, and the characteristic *r* sound is always clearly articulated in words like *car*.

While speakers of American or British English frequently drop or de-emphasise some syllables in longer words, South Indians are more likely to enunciate each syllable fully. So a South Indian would pronounce the word 'typical' as *ti·pi·khal* whereas a North Indian would say *tip·kal*. This also means that word endings will be more clearly articulated in words like *readiness* than they are in standard English.

The more familiar you are with the pronunciation rules of India's many regional languages, the more you'll appreciate the diversity of Indian English pronunciation across the country – and remember that the speakers' social status, class and educational background can influence their pronunciation as much as their region of origin. Indeed, it's now possible to speak of an educated Indian English accent as heard on news channels and in elite circles. To get an insight into some of the key regional differences, have a look at Lonely Planet's *India* phrasebook, which provides pronunciation guides for a good many local indigenous languages.

Grammar

It used to be claimed by some that the only rule of Indian English was that there were no rules, but times have changed. After all, the millions of Indian English speakers can't *all* be 'wrong', can they?

When speakers of other English varieties hear Indian English for the first time it might sound like grammatical anarchy, however the language does abide by consistent rules and conventions – they're just different from those of standard English.

To use a sporting analogy, rugby was 'invented' in 1823 when a schoolboy from Rugby in England by the name of William Webb Ellis broke the rules during a game of football (soccer) by picking up the ball and running towards goal. Naturally football players were pretty offended that the rules had been broken, but the end result was a new game with its own rules, which everyone enjoyed. So, just as rugby changed some of the rules of standard football to create a new game, Indians have picked up the English ball and run with it, without any sign of slowing!

WACKY VERBS

Verbs in Indian English can differ in weird and wonderful ways from verbs in standard English, most notably in their endings and the way they combine with other words.

THE VERY INDIAN MISS PUSHPA TS

The playful elegance of Indian English grammar shines through in the verse of Nissim Ezekiel, considered to be one of the founding fathers of Indian English poetry.

A member of Mumbai's Jewish-Indian community, his works have been studied at schools in both India and Britain. He died in 2004 at the age of 79 and is remembered for unashamedly using his native variety of English to develop the uniquely Indian characters that populate his writing.

Miss Pushpa is just one of his many celebrated examples. In the poem *Goodbye Party For Miss Pushpa TS*, the speaker describes his beloved Miss Pushpa who is **departing for foreign** (going abroad). He repeats the word 'smiling' to indicate that Miss Pushpa smiles frequently, and uses **Miss Pushpa will do summing up** to simply mean 'Miss Pushpa will sum up'.

Indian English verbs combine with prepositions (like 'on', 'for' and 'to') in ways that deviate from standard English: in some phrases, prepositions are casually abandoned, in others new prepositions are unexpectedly inserted. For example, Indians **carry out** their bags rather than 'carry' them. Likewise they **return back** their library books rather than 're-turn' them.

One of the most noticeable idiosyncrasies of Indian English is the frequent use of the '-ing' form of the verb. It's common to hear Indians utter phrases like **Always she is singing your praises** or perhaps **She is having two books** and even **You must be knowing my brother**.

Although some have accused Indian English speakers of flouting the rules of grammar, on closer inspection you'll discover that they are actually often just regularising the weird quirks of standard English. The 'irregular' adverbs of standard English, for example, are sometimes regularised in Indian English, so it's acceptable to say things like *She worked very hardly.*

Verbs are cooked up like homemade specials, simply by taking a verb in a local language and adding a standard English verb ending. The Hindi word *gao* (sing) can be made into *gaoing* (singing), while the Hindi word *masti* (fun) can become *mastify* (liven up), eg, *Arre, you should have seen her gaoing her teacher's praises!* and *Let's mastify this a bit, it's too dull.*

NIFTY NOUNS

Need a new noun? Start with a standard English ending like '-dom' (as in 'freedom') and '-ism' (as in 'racism') and add it to a local word to produce new expressions like *cooliedom* (from *coolie* 'porter') and *goondaism* (from *goonda* 'thug'). Indigenous endings are just as easily latched on to standard English nouns to create new terms, for example the Hindi ending '-ni' is used when talking to (or about) a woman, as in *daaktarni* (female doctor or a doctor's wife) and *masterni* (female school teacher).

Indian English nouns don't always combine in expected ways and it's quite common for people to refer to a *chalk piece* ('a piece of chalk') or even a *key bunch* ('bunch of keys').

MYRIAD SHADES OF 'BLACK'	
black	dark complexion
blacker	darker
blackened	reputation dragged through mud
black-black	jet black
black heart	having wicked thoughts
black deeds	cruelty
black face	ashamed
blackout	power failure or fainting

Nouns are sometimes unexpectedly plural, resulting in curious formulations like *a pile of litters*, *a room full of furnitures* and *woods for chopping*. At other times, words that are pluralised in standard English remain singular in Indian English in phrases such as *Yesterday one of my relative won the lottery*.

DISORDERLY WORD ORDER

One of the delights of learning to make sense of Indian English is getting used to sentences with seemingly jumbled up words. This apparent muddle is largely thanks to the fact that most Indian languages structure their sentences following a different pattern to standard English.

Stock-in-trade questions like 'When are they coming?', 'Who have you come for?' and 'What would you like to eat?' are put through the wringer of indigenous sentence structures and pop out the other side out as *When they are coming? Who you have come for?* and *What you would like to eat?*

A particularly tricky one for outsiders to get their heads around is the placement of 'all'. In more-logical-than-the-original Indian style, the word 'all' occurs just before the noun, resulting in sentences like *My all friends are waiting* and *Your all cupboards are empty*.

TAGGED, ISN'T IT?

In regional languages like Tamil, Kannada and Hindi, questions are always indicated with a 'tag' at the end, and speakers of Indian English imitate this principle. Throughout India the most universal question tag is *isn't it?* but other tags such as *right?* and *no?* are also common. Just as in standard English, question tags indicate that a question has been asked and that the speaker seeks confirmation for a point of view. The difference is that, in India, the tag doesn't have to correspond or 'agree' with the preceding phrase. This results in apparently incongruous questions like *He is very weak, isn't it? You have a job, isn't it?* and *He'll come back, isn't it?*

Vocabulary

Every year the lexicon of Indian English expands and its legitimacy has been given a further boost by the inclusion of Indian English words into the latest edition of the Oxford English Dictionary. Among the new additions are *Hinglish* (see box p8), *mehndi* (henna), *tom-tom* (drum), *off-shoring* (relocation of a business from one country to another), *prepone* (the reverse of postpone) and *agitation* (a public demonstration).

While almost all of the words used in Indian English are found in standard English, there are a number of terms that have been adopted directly from local indigenous languages. Below are a couple of the most common:

wallah is from a Hindi word meaning both 'person' and 'tradesperson' and is used to denote someone's occupation or involvement in an activity. A *paper-wallah* is a paperboy or someone who sells or distributes newspapers. An *icecream-wallah* sells ice cream and a *kerosene-wallah* sells kerosene, while cabbies are *taxi-wallahs* and a *grocery-wallah* is the man who sells groceries.

yaar is Hindi for 'friend' or 'buddy'. Stallholders might use this when looking to close a deal, as in, *Come on, yaar, this is very best price*.

Some of the most inventive items of vocabulary have come about without any apparent inspiration from elsewhere.

TALKING-SHALKING

Indians, especially North Indians, are big on 'echo' words tagged onto a noun. The results are 'sing-song' Indian English words that lend a playful rhythm to the spoken vernacular. These are used to enliven everyday conversation, eg *Too much meat-veat and no walking-shalking has made me fat*.

car-var	car
chai-shai	tea (and snacks) (from Hindi *chai* 'tea')
chair-vair	chair
chicken-shicken	chicken
dance-vance	dance
eating-veating	eating
fail-vail	fail
love-shove	love
marriage-sharriage	marriage
meat-veat	meat
talking-shalking	talking
train-vain	train
walking-shalking	walking

Abbreviations such as *fundas* (fundamentals) abound, as do acronyms like *ATKT* which stands for 'Allowed To Keep Terms' – the name for a special exam in the college jargon of Mumbai.

Indian English speakers have a nifty knack of breaking down standard English words and reformulating them to create new meanings. Prefixes like 'pre-', 'post-' and 're-' are prime candidates for such tailoring. The word *prepone*, mentioned earlier, is a logical derivation of 'postpone' and has the exact opposite meaning. So an Indian might say *The wedding has been preponed since the girl's parents can now afford a bigger dowry*.

Rhyming double-barreled words, like the ever-popular *ice-cream-fice-cream* (ice cream), and *fighting-shiting* (wrangling) are a unique and playful feature of Indian English (see box above).

BORROWINGS

Indian English functions like a busy two-way bridge between standard English and local Indian languages. Over the past decades, regional languages have borrowed many English terms, often when a suitable local substitute is unavailable. So when an Indian speaking their native language uses English words like *lorry*, *bus*, *car*, *stereo*, *TV*, *AC*, *mobile* and *radio*, it might be that the equivalent doesn't exist in their mother tongue, often the case for new technologies. For words which do have an equivalent, it might be that these sound socially backward or are complicated compounds. Punjabi, for example, has adopted reams of English words, such as *college*, *city*, *school*, and *thanks*.

In the same spirit, standard English has benefited from an influx of regional Indian terms, and loan words like *guru*, *nirvana*, *yoga* and *avatar* have almost mystically positioned themselves as English words. How many of the following exotic terms are familiar?

blighty   England (from Hindi *vilayati* 'foreign')

bungalow   a small house or cottage (from Hindi *bangala*)

catamaran   a boat with two parallel hulls or floats (from Tamil *kettumaram*, from *kettu* 'to tie' and *maram* 'wood')

cheroot   a cigar with square cut ends (from Tamil *churuttu* 'roll of tobacco leaves')

coir   fibre from the outer husk of the coconut, used in potting compost and for making ropes and matting (from Malayalam *kayaru* 'cord')

cot   portable bed (from Hindi *khaat* 'bed')

crore   10 million (from Hindi *karor*)

cushy   comfortable (from Hindi *kushi* 'happy')

dacoit   robber (from Hindi *dacait*)

dinghy   small boat (from Hindi or Bengali *dingi*)

dungaree   workman's overalls (from Hindi *dungri*)

jungle   forest, wilds (from Hindi *jangala* 'forest')

loot   to pillage (from Hindi *lut*, originally from Sanskrit *loptrum/lotrum* plunder)

pukka great, fine, respectable (from Hindi *pakka*, 'cooked, ripe')

teak hard durable timber used in shipbuilding and for making furniture, native to India and southeast Asia (via Portuguese *teca*, from Tamil/Malayalam *tekku*)

thug tough and violent man (from Hindi *thag* 'thief')

IDIOMATICALLY SPEAKING

Indian English is bursting with colloquial sayings and expressions. With so many linguistic influences working to shape it, it's no surprise there are some real gems when it comes to idiomatic language in all domains of society. Indian merchants, for instance, are fond of *OTT* (over the top) exaggerations of quantity and there is no denying the regular use of *99.9%*, *101%* or even *200%*, however mathematically challenged these expressions are. Office workplaces and social hangouts are also fertile soil for new expressions.

Here are some favourites:

I got a firing	I was yelled at, eg *I went to work and I got a firing from the boss.*
cheap and best	good value, eg *That masala was cheap and best, no?*
join duty	to report to work for the first time, and to *rejoin duty* is to return to work from vacation
go for a toss	go haywire or go wrong, eg *It was a disaster, everything went for a toss.*
on the anvil	something is about to happen, eg *A promotion is on the anvil.*

Twisted turns of phrase surface in Indian English as literal translations of common phrases in regional languages. Here are just a few:

close the light	switch off the light
open the light	switch on the light
don't eat my head	don't irritate me
put the tape	play the tape
give a test	write a test
take tea	drink tea
take bath	bathe

THE WHOLE STORY

Indian English draws inspiration from the nation's rich spiritual past. If you want a peek at the most popular Indian English phrases of the future, get hold of a copy of the 24,000 verse holy Sanskrit epic known as the *Ramayana* (see box p70). The venerated 2,000 year old tale is responsible for these modern-day Indian English sayings:

lakshman rekha crossing the *lakshman rekha* (literally 'Lakshman's line'), is to cross the limit at your own peril. In the epic *Ramayana*, Lakshman has to leave his sister-in-law Sita alone to go looking for his brother Rama, so he marks a magical line around her hut to protect her as long as she stays within it. Alas, she was tricked into crossing the line (for good reason) and thereby hangs a tale…

ram kahani the whole story (literally 'Rama's story', a reference to the *Ramayana*)

who is Sita? asking a basic question, as in 'you listened to the whole *Ramayana* and now ask who is Sita!' Sita is the much-revered wife of Lord Rama.

INTERJECTIONS

Indians are open and quick to make friends and this is reflected in their use of interjections to generate intimacy during conversations. You'll know you're amongst friends if you start hearing some of these expressions:

achchha means 'good' but can also be used to express surprise, eg *Achchha, what a nightmare!* (Hindi)

arre means 'hey', eg *Arre! That's fantastic!* (Hindi)

chal literally means 'walk'; it can be used loosely in the sense 'let's go' or colloquially to indicate agreement, eg *Chal, I'm coming* (Hindi)

theek hai used in place of OK, it roughly means 'all right' (Hindi)

uff indicates distress, concern or frustration, as in *Uff! Not curry again!* (Hindi/Urdu)

wah use this to show your appreciation especially at a performance, eg *Wah, you're a demon on the dholak* (side drum; Urdu)

Meeting & greeting

As a rule Indian English is fairly informal – the major exception is with meetings and greetings. The practice of shaking hands, which was once mocked as a British affectation, is now standard etiquette for business meetings in India.

MAD OR WHAT?

When Indian English speakers want to strike a casual chord, they'll smatter their sentences with *I see*, *I know*, *man*, *ya* (from *yaar* 'buddy'), *na* ('no') and similar interjections. *You know what* is another favourite opener along with *And* as in *And, how's life?* Standard responses of disbelief range from *As if!* to *Mad or what?*

Anyone from a profession considered to be prestigious, such as a doctor or professor, would expect that you use their title as a matter of respect. If you don't know someone's title, the safest option is to use a generic term which is why you will often be greeted as 'sir' or 'madam' by Indians, for whom a polite greeting is not so much an act of formality as a display of good manners.

Respect is imperative when it comes to Indian greetings. The *-ji* in **Hello-ji, how are you?** is a marker of respect for addressing women, elders or anyone worthy of deference. The ending *-ji* also follows names when referring to someone who is highly regarded, eg **It's a pleasure meeting you, Gupta-ji**.

Those with a good ear for names will be one step ahead in social interactions in India as names often provide important clues to a person's background and social standing. For example, Bengalis whose names end in 'jee' (eg **Banerjee**) are likely to be Hindu, while the ending 'kar' (eg **Chandraskar**) marks a place of origin for Maharashtrians. Someone called **Singh** is likely to be a Sikh but the name is also common for Rajputs and Thakurs. The names **Dwivedi**, **Trivedi** and **Chaturvedi** indicate that the people's ancestors read two, three and four Vedas (ancient Hindu scriptures) respectively.

ADDRESS TERMS
Indian English speakers have access to a broad vocabulary of respect terms derived from local languages and standard English. Here are some common ways to address people in India:

anna elder brother or any older male (Tamil)

aunty this follows a name and is used to address any older woman, eg *Let me help you with those heavy bags, Sarita Aunty*

baba another one to use with older people, this title translates as 'father' and is used when addressing older men (Urdu)

ben address to a Gujurati woman, literally 'sister'. It can be used by itself or tagged onto names, eg *Sushila-ben.* (Gujarati)

bhai/bhaiyya literally 'brother', these respectful terms are used in a similar way to 'dude' or 'man' in other varieties of English. The term *bhaiyya* is slightly more informal and affectionate. Eg *Come on bhai, it'll be cool* or *It's been a while, bhaiyya* (Hindi)

boss a colloquial address to colleagues irrespective of status

da term of respect for elder brother or any older male in West Bengal (Bengali)

di term of respect for older sister or any older female in West Bengal (Bengali)

missus/Mrs title of respect for a woman or colloquial term for 'wife', eg *Is your missus in town?*

TERMS OF ENDEARMENT

Couples are sometimes coy about using one another's name in public and may choose to refer to each other as their child's father or mother, eg *Chunnu ke papa* (Chunnu's papa) and *Bunty ki ammi* (Bunty's mother) meaning 'my husband' and 'my wife' respectively.

mister/Mr title of respect for a man or colloquial term for 'husband', eg *My mister is very loving*

sahib/saab follows a man's name to show respect, as in ***Welcome home Smith-sahib***; it is also a term of address, eg ***Where do you want to go, sahib?*** (Urdu)

Shri equivalent of 'Mr', eg ***Shri Ravi Shankar*** (Hindi)

Shrimati equivalent of 'Mrs', eg ***Shrimati Das Gupta*** (Hindi)

uncle this follows a name and can be used to address any older man, including relatives, neighbours, and total strangers. For example, ***Thanks for coming, Chandra Uncle***.

HELLOS
Greetings and salutatory blessings in Indian English vary depending on what part of the country you are in, your religious background and your native language. These are some common phrases:

adaab hello, literally 'respect' (Urdu, Arabic origin)

ayushman bhava live long (Sanskrit)

chiranjivi live forever (Tamil)

jai (ho) (may there be) victory (Hindi)

namaste/namaskaram I bow to you (it is accompanied by a slight bow and the hands pressed together in a prayer-like gesture; Hindi)

pai lagoo respectful greeting used in the more remote northern villages, literally 'feet touch' (accompanied by a foot-touching gesture; Hindi)

salam peace (Urdu, Arabic origin)

sat sri akal truth is God (Punjabi)

vale-kum-salam peace be with you (Urdu, Arabic origin)

vanakam welcome (Tamil)

GOODBYES

For Indian English speakers it is considered bad luck to say goodbye with finality. It is much better to say ***see you later***, ***until we meet again***, ***I will return***, ***I am coming back soon*** or even simply ***I'll go and come back***. The promise to return is meant to ward off the evil eye, which may be cast if a categorical statement of departure with no mention of a return is made.

chalta hoon	literally 'I'll walk' (Hindi)
jai hind	victory to India (Hindi)
khuda hafiz	goodbye, literally 'may God protect you' (Urdu)
make a move	as in ***I'll make a move, it is getting late***
phir milenge	meet you later (Hindi)
pogalam	I'll leave (Tamil)
Ram-Ram	chanting of Lord Rama's name, also used as a greeting. The reply to ***Ram-Ram*** is also ***Ram-Ram***.
take your leave	eg ***allow me to take your leave now*** (a formal-sounding phrase used by Indians in quite informal situations)

Being polite

As with any language variety, some expressions in Indian English are more polite than others, and it's important to know which is which to avoid embarrassment. Hotel guests might be asked *What is your good name?* by the receptionist which is not some vestige of yesteryear's British English but a literal translation of the Hindi phrase *Aapka shubh naam kya hai?*

Sometimes the level of politeness of a given turn of phrase in Indian English is different to standard English. For example, the phrase *you people* risks coming across as aggressive but it's simply a direct translation of the perfectly polite Hindi expression *aap log,* which means 'you' (plural) in standard English. The expression *Hello, what you want?* is a standard way of answering the phone but is easily misread as rudeness by non-Indians. On the other hand terms that may be neutral in standard English have stronger and more negative connotations in Indian English. The word *rowdy,* for example, implies criminal behaviour.

Gestures & body language

Borrowing liberally from street theatre, stage and screen, Indians may deliver sudden taps, abrupt winks, and perhaps even a painful abdominal nudge, all in the interest of 'picturesque' speech. Nods, shrugs (with either one or both shoulders), exaggerated blinks, sudden aerial arcs of the hands, an open-shut movement of the palms (to negate) and clenched fists are part of the pantomime.

blinks and shrugs   expresses negation

click of tongue   is used to negate or sympathise

head nod   indicates listening

palm covering cheek   conveys exaggerated sympathy or shock

patting tummy   shows hunger pangs (a favourite gesture among beggars who know that verbal communication with foreigners is difficult)

shrug accompanied by a verbal click   conveys ignorance

shaking head   negates

thumb and forefinger pointing from clenched hand   is used to question why, where, when, who, or how

---

WIBBLE WOBBLE

The characteristic head wobbling beloved of Indians everywhere is far from gratuitous. Whenever a speaker is wobbling their head, attention needs to be given to the direction and intensity of the wobble – this provides important signals about their intended meaning. Wobbling the head from side to side signals that the listener is paying attention. If the movement turns to nodding, however, the speaker is either adding emphasis to a point they've just made or they are agreeing with something the listener just said. The speed and arc of the nod usually indicate the amount of emphasis or agreement. Meanwhile, a shake of the head represents either disagreement or draws attention to the fact that a question has been asked.

When Indians in rural areas have an argument over a small matter, there can be a fair amount of physical proximity between them if the row becomes heated. They probably won't resort to actual violence – it's just part of the nonverbal communication. In the north, a good argument is preceded by the rolling up of sleeves, while in the south, the bottom half of the *lungi* (traditional pants) is shaken loose and retied at the waist.

In India it is possible to pay a tremendous compliment with body language alone. When somebody approaches a person with their tongue between their teeth and gathers the air around the person's head with their hands to draw it into their own personal space, it means they find the person either unbearably beautiful or extraordinarily intelligent. This is the way to ward off the evil eye.

Men touching women, even with the most platonic of intents, is a strict no-no outside the metros and large cities. In remote areas, the presence of a male guest brings on the **ghoongat** (semi-purdah), where the sari's **pallu** (veil) is demurely drawn over a woman's face. When a male guest is in the presence of a veiled woman, the protocol is to address queries to male counterparts only.

Elderly people are particularly venerated in the villages. When a youth greets an elderly person, it is expected that they also touch their feet. Then the older person will mouth blessings in their mother tongue, like *May you live a thousand years!* or *May you be the mother of one hundred sons!* Other traditional blessings include *jeete raho* (live forever) or *sada sukhi raho* (always be happy).

While conversing in Indian English, it is important to maintain eye contact with your audience. Of course, this is good manners in a number of cultures, including the West, but especially so in India. Paying attention to the face also means you won't miss out on any relevant hand gestures. Key statements are often accompanied by dramatic gestures. *Oh my goodness!* is rarely uttered without an accompanying slap to the cheek just to make sure the listener appreciates the seriousness of the situation.

I PROMISE

Indians promise, pledge, and vow with vigour, and a number of different types of promises are articulated with accompanying movements. Brushing the head with a finger is known as a *Sar ki kasam* ('head promise' in Hindi). The gesture literally implies that if the speaker is lying their head will roll off. As a rule, the promise is performed without the accompanying phrase.

Other prominent promises involve stooping to touch mud (Mother Earth) for a *ma kasam* (mother promise) or pinching the skin of one's neck as you carry out a *meri kasam* (I promise on myself), which is the equivalent of saying 'cross my heart and hope to die' in other varieties of English.

India is booming. The romantic image of an enchanted land full of wild tigers and smug cattle, its cities peopled with snake charmers sitting cross-legged beside *yogis* sleeping on beds of nails, while widows jump onto their husband's funeral pyre to commit *sati* (self-immolation), has gradually modernised as the country hurls itself into the 21st century.

Nowadays the snake charmers have mobile phones and the yogis are masters of business management as well as the *adho mukha svanasana* (downward-facing dog pose). The *metros* (big cities) and smaller cities boast call centres servicing customers as far away as Europe, the USA and Australia. Such businesses have been instrumental in creating a hip, youthful Indian middle class. Ambitious, degree-qualified executives have money to spend and are challenging traditional values while powering Western-style consumerism. According to the latest figures available, the number of new internet users increased in India in 2006 by 33 per cent to over 21 million. It was the highest growth rate in internet usage worldwide.

Poverty, however, remains the country's biggest challenge. More than a quarter of the population subsists below the poverty line, with the majority of these people living in rural villages. Desperate villagers flock to nearby cities, which lack the infrastructure to support them. Even some smaller cities, like Ranchi in the picturesque Chota Nagpur Valley, have had trouble coping with these new arrivals and now have large slums. As a consequence, improving the quality of village life to encourage people to stay has become a priority for government in India at every level.

Lifestyle & society

That said, the modernisation of the country and growth of the middle class can't be stopped. Increasingly, advertisements for *ayurveda* (alternative medicine) health spas, beach holidays, and sightseeing tours to rust-hued deserts are aimed more at the Indian middle class than at visiting foreigners. The old stereotype of India as a backward, densely populated 'quaint' destination, popular with *chillum* (drug-smoking pipe) charged hippies, will probably always remain, but the signs that the country will soon be a global superpower are everywhere.

In the shadow of a skyscraper, the *metropolitan* (big city) man with product-coated hair co-exists with the bow-legged *rickshaw-puller*. The single working girl sashays past a beggar while talking to a friend on her mobile phone about the impact international politics is having on petrol prices. The palmist who promises to predict your future is evicted from his home in the slums that are being bulldozed to make way for a new up-market leisure centre. It's all happening right here, right now.

India has always been a land of economic and social extremes; fascinating because it is a country of contradictions. It is said that every day you spend in India, you should expect the unexpected. Perhaps this is why a place renowned as one of the most chaotic on earth is also the land most closely associated with *nirvana* (enlightenment).

Types of people

India was a ruthlessly class-based society long before Britain imposed its unique brand of snobbery upon it. Long after the British have gone, divisions between rich and poor, rural and city, higher caste and lower caste, Hindu and Muslim now continue, as before, to shape hearts and minds, not to mention life chances. The brand of clothes you wear is vitally important, even more so than in the West, and instantly assigns your place in the socio-economic hierarchy. And, in the absence of such material markers, speech sends clear signals about everything from education levels, career aspirations, and the extent of one's 'Indianness'.

Throughout the country, many different languages and regional dialects can be heard. It is in the huge cities, or *metros*, like Mumbai, Kolkata, and Delhi where the cacophony of different languages is most intense. Indian English cuts across linguistic, cultural and geographical divides by providing a single medium of communication in many situations where people share no other common language.

Cities, large and small, are densely packed with kaleido-scopic ethnic and cultural diversity, which is reflected in the following terms:

adivasi   the various tribal people who comprise a substantial indigenous minority in India (Hindi)

awam   people (Urdu)

bhadralok   the educated cultural elite of Bengal (Bengali)

country cousin   someone hailing from the same state or village as you

Dalit   an *Untouchable* – a person outside the caste system, who is considered to be of very low social status (Hindi, literally 'oppressed')

devadasi   prostitute, from Sanskrit 'servant of god' – a euphemism for prostitution sanctioned by the Hindu faith

---

SOCIAL PARIAHS

A *pariah* is 'a social outcast', though formerly in South India it also meant 'a member of a low caste'. The word originally comes from Tamil *paraiyan* meaning 'drummer' because members of this caste were traditionally the drummers at festivals. The word was first recorded in English in 1613.

Gulf Malayalee   Indians working in the Persian Gulf region, the majority of which come from Kerala, a state where Malayalam is spoken

Harijan   a term coined by Mahatma Gandhi to dignify the lower castes, who were until then called *Untouchables* (Hindi, literally 'god's people')

kabuli-wallah   pedlar from Afghanistan – immortalised by Rabindranath Tagore in the short story *Kabuli-wallah*

maharaja   great Hindu princely ruler (Hindi)

maharani   a *maharaja's* wife (Hindi)

pahari   a term used to refer to any mountain-dwelling people in India; in North India it specifically refers to people dwelling in the Himalayas (Hindi)

Parsi   followers of *Zoroastrianism* (a monotheistic religion), *Parsis* are descendants of the Zoroastrians who migrated to India in 936 AD from Persia

raja   a king (Hindi)

rajkumar   a prince (Hindi)

rajkumari   a princess (Hindi)

rani   a queen or princess (the wife of a *raja*) (Hindi)

rajput   sons of rulers (Hindi)

sadhu   a wandering Hindu holy man (Hindi)

Sardar   males of the Sikh religion have this title (Urdu)

Sardarni   a title used to refer to Sikh women (Urdu)

sherpa   a people from the east (Tibetan)

veshya   a prostitute (Hindi)

Country versus city

India's traditionally small-scale agrarian economy is in decline, and its cities are ever expanding. Farmers and their sons would rather migrate to the nearby towns and cities than tend to *kheti-baadi* (farms). While urban idealists wax lyrical about unspoilt paradises and the benefits of a basic subsistence lifestyle, the reality for members of the older generation who choose to remain on the land is that they often feel trapped and lonely, and abandoned by their children, who are seeking out greener pastures in the industrialised cities. *Paathshalas* (schools) and *panchayats* (local representative bodies) struggle to survive the exodus. Ironically, the city-based middle classes are beginning to rediscover the charms of rural life and, come the weekend, office workers take flight to the *gaanvs* (villages) champing at the bit to brush their teeth with *neem* (herbal) twigs and eat *bajra* (coarse grain) *rotis*. Quaint as village life may seem, the city slickers seldom forget to bring their bottles of mineral water with them when visiting.

DARK MATTER

The term *Anglo-Indian* technically designates a descendant of mixed British and Indian lineage, although it now describes a person of any mixed European-Indian blood. Many Anglo-Indians are, in fact, of Portuguese origin. British English is the mother tongue of this relatively small community, which has two nominated members appointed in the *Lok Sabha*, the lower house of the Indian parliament, because the community has no native state of its own.

India's ethnic mix has spawned a hierarchy of skin tone in Indian English vocabulary. *Wheatish skin* refers to a light-brown complexion. Any pigmentation *above* (lighter than) *wheatish* is described as *fair*, *very fair* or even *white* (pronounced 'bhyte' by Bengalis with strong regional accents). More tanned skin is *dark* (see also boxed text p47).

VILLAGE PEOPLE

Despite the current trend of people moving to the city, there are still many villages where water is drawn from *kuan* (wells), the *sabzis* (vegetables) are wholesome and fresh, and night-time brings out *mombatti* (candles) or *petromax* (gas lights). *Bijli* (electricity) is still not available in some villages.

Respect for elders is a characteristic of village life. The toothless elderly citizens are referred to as *buzurg* (learned elderly) or *bade boode* (literally 'the great old'). The younger generation is scornfully nicknamed *bachche* (children) when they're being *nadaan* (ignorant). When youths are being derided for their big city aspirations you might hear them refer to the *buzurg* as a bunch of *ganwaars* (illiterates) or *angootha-chhaaps* (those who sign with a thumbprint) who only know how to smoke their *hookahs* (home-made clay pipes).

The following words are commonly heard around the village:

anganwadi   a rural crèche (literally 'courtyard play centre', Hindi)

chit fund   an investment fund formed between a group of people – loosely regulated and informal (Indian English)

cow-dung cakes   dried cow-dung patties used as a cooking fuel (Indian English)

dai   a midwife; now health services are increasingly found in villages but earlier midwives would come to deliver a baby (Urdu)

gobar gas   methane gas produced from cow dung or compost (Hinglish, from Hindi *gobar* 'cow dung' and English *gas*)

mofussil   far from big cities (Urdu)

panchayat   the body of representatives who make decisions about a village's social, cultural or economic life (Hindi)

village daughter   a woman born in a particular village as opposed to one who came in by marriage (Indian English)

zamindar   landowner in a village (Urdu)

zenana   the women's quarters in a Muslim household (Urdu)

CITY DWELLERS

City life is synonymous with speed, affluence and careering down the fast lane. Those who get ahead are turned out *tip-top* (stylish), attend a *hairdresser* rather than a *hajaam* (barber) and indulge in *nightlife* (bars and late-night shows). India's five major cities, Delhi (the richest and national capital), Mumbai (the commercial and entertainment capital, formerly Bombay), Bengaluru (the Silicon Valley of India, formerly

---

SUPERSTITIOUS WAYS

Long before feng shui started catching on in India, and before *Vaastu Shastra* (the Vedic science of architecture) or tarot card reading caught on, Indians were comforted with horoscopes, *upais* (celestial remedies), *jyotishis* (astrologers), *pundits* (learned Brahmins) and palmists galore. Superstitions in Indian culture stem from all areas of life: religion, psychology, old wives' tales or even a sneeze. Bollywood film-makers like Karan Johar and TV moguls like Ektaa Kapoor famously perpetuate the *K-Name Syndrome*, that only movies whose titles begin with the letter 'K' have any chance of success. All manner of superstition is alive and well in modern-day India. Left eye twitching? Someone's gossiping about you. Left palm itching? You're going to come into money. An upturned shoe indicates you're about to lose some money. But don't get worried, just chant a mantra and you'll have nothing to worry about.

Bangalore), Chennai (formerly Madras) and Kolkata (formerly Calcutta), are referred to as *metros*.

The drive or walk into a centre is known as *going to town*. Unlike in the rest of the English-speaking world, however, any place which has some development, such as markets, eateries, beaches or even just a school, can qualify as a *town*. Many *townspeople* live in *flats*, which are usually small apartments, such as those built in Delhi by the *DDA* (Delhi Development Authority).

Following are some words commonly heard in the big cities and towns:

baniya a shopkeeper or someone of a trading caste; it is sometimes used derogatorily for someone who is materialistic (Hindi)

bhikhari a beggar (Hindi)

burning ghat a place of cremation (Hinglish)

calling bell a doorbell (Indian English)

chaalu working, running (eg of a machine); used derogatorily for a *fast* (loose) or indecent woman (Hindi)

city can mean anything from the tiniest village to a big town or a small or large city (Indian English)

dhobi/dhobin a laundry man/woman (Hindi)

good status an adjective used to describe a well-to-do person (Indian English)

localites residents of a particular place (Indian English)

native place one's place of origin (Indian English)

oldies elderly people (Indian English)

pagal mad, as in *Don't be pagal!* (Hindi)

picture a movie (Indian English)

Puppies upwardly mobile Punjabi yuppies (Indian English)

quarter plate   a side dish (Indian English)

service   employment, job, as in 'I do service' (Indian English)

shifting house   moving house (Indian English)

suburbs   satellite townships of a major city, eg Gurgaon near Delhi, Vashi near Mumbai and Hebbal near Bengaluru (Indian English)

underworld   refers to the dark crime nexus in a city's underbelly (Indian English)

vela   unemployed, as in *I'll come with you as I am vela* (Hindi)

veranda   a porch sometimes running along the exterior of a building (from Hindi *beraamda* 'railing')

whatnot   a shelving unit for displaying random bric-a-brac-like crockery and curios (Indian English)

YOUNGSPEAK

Teenagers *flip* for the opposite sex, *click* with each other, *bunk* or *cut* (miss) classes to go to the movies, contact *dalals* (brokers) to buy a secondhand motorbike or *PG (paying-guest) digs* (rental accommodation). They aspire to get cushy jobs and may shower *shabaashi* (praise) on *nautchgirls* (dancing girls) in dance bars, or go abroad for *higher studies*. They say *rubber* for erasers and condoms alike, and tell each other they have *pulled down* (look exhausted) or *gone down* (have lost weight) as they don their *keds* (sneakers) and write in *India ink* (jet black ink) to their *Miss* (teacher) about how inspired they are by her *love marriage*. Meanwhile, the unpopular kid will find himself labelled a *lech* (lecherous individual) and be regarded by his peers as *shady* and perhaps a bit of a *shiznit* (weirdo).

HOUSEHOLD NAMES

Mahatma Gandhi   (1869–1948)

Also known as *Bapuji* (an affectionate term for 'father') or the *Father of the Nation*, Mohandas Karamchand Gandhi had a leading role in India's independence movement when he defeated the British with his unique *ahimsa* (nonviolence) movement. He was shot dead by a political dissenter on 30 January 1948, now annually commemorated as *Martyr's Day*.

Jawaharlal Nehru   (1889–1964)

Nehru was the first prime minister of independent India and governed from 1947 until his death in 1964. His birthday, 14 November, is now celebrated as *Children's Day*, as he was affectionately called Chacha (Uncle) Nehru by children.

Rabindranath Tagore   (1861–1941)

A prolific Bengali writer across many genres who won the Nobel Prize for Literature for his collection of poems *Gitanjali* (translated as *Song Offerings*) in 1913. An extremely learned man, he was also a social reformer, an educationalist, a participant in the Indian independence movement and a close friend of Mahatma Gandhi.

Mother Teresa   (1910–1997)

Popularly known as the *Angel of Mercy* and *Saint of the Gutter*, Mother Teresa, born Agnes Gonxha Bojaxhiu in Macedonia in 1910, came to India at the age of 19 to join the Sisters of Loreto and, at age 39, with the Pope's blessing, she founded the Sisters of Charity to serve Kolkata's poor. In 1979 she was awarded the Nobel Peace Prize. She passed away 5 September 1997 and has since been beatified by the Roman Catholic Church.

Indira Gandhi   (1917–1984)

The daughter of Jawaharlal Nehru (and no relation to Mahatma Gandhi), Indira Gandhi became prime minister in

1966 and defeated the *goongi gudiya* (dumb doll) tag by proving to be a forceful, and, at times, heavy-handed leader. In 1984, while still in office, she was shot dead in her garden by two of her Sikh security guards.

Kalpana Chawla (1961–2003)
The Indian-born astronaut Kalpana Chawla lost her life when NASA's space shuttle Columbia disintegrated in 2003 while re-entering the earth's atmosphere. She's remembered in her hometown of Karnal in the state of Haryana as having reached for the stars and staying there. She has an enduring legacy as a hero and role model for many young Indian people, especially women.

Phoolan Devi (1963–2001)
The *Bandit Queen* of the Chambal Valley, Uttar Pradesh, allegedly killed 22 *thakurs* (high-caste landlords) for gang raping her. She eventually surrendered to police and, after being imprisoned for 11 years without charge, became a politician. She was popularly regarded as the champion of the downtrodden. Phoolan Devi herself fiercely disputed the accuracy of the 1993 Shekhar Kapur film about her life, *Bandit Queen*, even seeking to have it banned in India. She was gunned down in front of her New Delhi home in 2001.

JRD Tata (1904–1993)
A French-born Parsi businessman who established India's first air service, Tata Aviation, which later became the government-owned airline Air India. He was founder and director of the huge Tata Group, which has major interests in many industries in India including the steel, engineering, hospitality and electrical sectors, and has recently produced the world's cheapest car. He was famous for succeeding in business whilst maintaining high ethical standards, refusing to bribe politicians.

Clothing & fashion

A thriving fashion industry with its beauty contests, *modelling shows*, skin-whitening *fairness creams* and *ramp walking* (walking the catwalk) propels into use Indian English words like *border* (the design on sari or skirt borders), *maxi* (a full-length frock) and *nighty* (a house gown worn at any time of the day).

In the big smoke, people with *city-groomed looks* are described as *suited-booted*, *gora sahib* (European), *memsahib* (literally 'madam'), *tip-top*, *first-class* or *first-rate* – all of which roughly equate to 'fashionable' or 'sophisticated'. Men seek to embellish their good looks with a *French beard* (a small goatee). Women have the option of wearing their hair short, a practice anathema in most rural areas.

Colour still has connotations steeped more in cultural tradition than in the fleeting fashions of the catwalks of Milan. *Lal* (red) is for *dulhan* (brides), and *safed* (white) is for *vidhwa* (widows), although the once strict hierarchies of hues have now been relaxed.

India has long been one of the world's great textile centres and has contributed a number of words to standard English. How many of these do you own?

bandana	headscarf (Hindi)
bangle	a bracelet or anklet (Hindi)
cummerbund	a broad sash (Urdu, from Farsi)
dungarees	trousers or overalls made of denim (place name)
jodhpurs	breeches used for horse riding (place name)
khakis	trousers made from traditional cloth (Urdu, from Farsi)
pyjamas	sleepwear (Urdu, from Farsi)
pashmina	lightweight Kashmiri shawls (Urdu, from Farsi)

At home *almirahs* (cupboards) overflow with basic clothing such as *jootis* (enclosed sandals) and *jholas* (cloth bags) as well as *khadi* (spun cotton) clothes and *kolhapuris* (flat brown sandals from Kolhapur in Maharashtra) for *aam* (ordinary) life. Night-time sees the *cham-cham* (glittery) stuff come out for the *party-sharties* (parties).

In Indian English, the word *dress* refers to clothing for all genders. This makes India one of the few places where straight men will proudly tell you they 'bought a new dress'. *Home-clothes* are clothes worn solely at home. So, if someone tells you about a woman who 'wore home-clothes to the party' the person in question has zero fashion sense. Some people make no distinction between the words 'cloth' and 'clothes', which are used interchangeably, for example *waste-cloth* refers to clothes that are not wearable. Clothes are either stitched at *tailor-shops* or *ready-mades* bought from the shops.

Here are some less familiar Indian English words every fashionista should know:

achkan   a man's long-sleeved button-up tunic worn down to the knees (Hindi)

bandgala   a man's tunic with a high collar buttoned up to the neck (Hindi)

baniyan   an inner, sleeveless vest (Hindi)

bead-work   beaded embroidery (Indian English)

bell-bots   flared trousers, bell-bottoms (Indian English)

bindi   the ritual dot worn on the forehead by women (Hindi)

blouse   a short tunic worn with a sari (Indian English)

boy-cut   short hair on a girl (Indian English)

bush-shirt   a formal short-sleeved shirt (Indian English)

chappals   sandals (Hindi)

choli   a short-sleeved bodice, usually with elaborate embroidery, worn by women, especially with *saris* (Hindi)

chunni   a scarf worn over the shoulder with a *salwar-kameez* (Hindi)

churidar   pants that are baggy from the waist to the knee but tight from the knee down ending in *churis* (baggy cuffs, literally 'bangles') at the ankles (Hindi)

darzi   a tailor (Urdu)

dhoti   a long loincloth worn by men (Hindi)

dupatta   the same as a *chunni* (Hindi)

full-pant   trousers (Indian English)

ganji   a short vest (Hindi)

ghaghra   an ankle-length skirt (Hindi)

ghoonghat   a veil worn to display modesty (Hindi)

ghungroo   belled anklets (for dance) (Hindi)

half-pant   shorts (Indian English)

half-sari   a stole over a long skirt and blouse (Indian English)

henna   a natural plant-derived dye (Urdu, from Farsi)

jhola   a large shoulder bag associated with journalists and activists (Hindi)

jhumka   traditional dangly bell-shaped earrings in silver or gold (Hindi)

kajal   kohl (eyeliner) (Hindi)

kameez   a long shirt or tunic worn as part of a *salwar-kameez* (Urdu) *khadi*   hand-woven and hand-spun cotton (Hindi)

kum-kum   *bindi* powder (Hindi)

kundan   gold wire work used to decorate clothing, such as *sari* borders (Hindi)

kurti   a waist-length or thigh-length tunic (Hindi)

langot   a loincloth (Hindi)

lehenga   a dressy, decorative ankle-length skirt (Urdu)

lungi   a *dhoti* with coloured designs (Urdu)

lungi-pants   pants in the shape of a *lungi* (Hinglish, from *lungi*)

madras checks   a patterned cloth where the colours run across columns with each wash (Indian English)

mal   voile cloth (Urdu)

meena work   coloured enamel work (Hinglish, from Hindi *meena* 'enamel')

mirror work   pieces of mirrored glass used to decorate clothing (Indian English)

mokash   tiny sequins (Urdu)

Nehru jacket   a coat style favoured by the late prime minister Jawaharlal Nehru and marked with a high round collar (Indian English)

MY BOTTOM IS MISSING!

Sometimes items of clothing which are plural in other varieties of English, turn up in the singular in Indian English. For example, *pant* for pants, *trouser* for trousers. The lower half of outfits – *salwar*, *churidar*, *pant* and *sharara* – are called *bottom* for convenience. So, you might hear, *Where's my bottom?* or *I want a black bottom!* or even *My bottom is missing!*

pagdi   a turban (Hindi)

pallu   the flowing, graceful end of a *sari* (Hindi)

paper silk   a type of hand-loomed silk (Indian English)

Patiala salwar   loose pants gathered at the ankles (Urdu; *Patiala* is place name)

payal   an anklet (Hindi)

purdah   a burka (the long garment worn by Muslim women in public) (Urdu)

salwar   loose, gathered trousers (Urdu)

salwar-kameez   a long tunic worn with loose gathered trousers by men and women (women wear it with a *chunni/dupatta*) (Urdu)

sari   traditional female garment (Hindi)

underskirt   a skirt worn under a *sari* (Indian English)

zari   gold or silver work, especially on *sari* borders (Urdu)

Home & family

The average family size in India has been whittled down to four in the wake of the popular 1970s slogan *hum do, hamare do* (we two, our two). The main shift has been from the *joint family* (extended family) – where mothers, fathers, grandmothers, grandfathers, aunts, uncles, nieces, nephews, and children all reside together – to the nuclear family, consisting of just parents and their children. The old-fashioned hankering for a male heir to *carry the family name forward* still contributes, however, to large family sizes, particularly among the poor.

FAMILY TERMS

Trying to negotiate your way through all the terms for a standard Indian household can be a real challenge. The names for grandparents and most aunts and uncles are different in many Indian languages depending on whether they are related to one's mother or father. An encyclopaedic knowledge of the family tree is a prerequisite before you can ascribe monikers, such as those below, to their rightful owners. Just to confuse things, children often call strangers by the English terms uncle and aunty as a sign of respect.

abba	father (Urdu)
baba	father (Bengali)
bahu	daughter-in-law (Hindi)
bua	father's sister (Hindi)
behan	sister (Hindi)
chachi	father's brother's wife (Hindi)
co-brother-in-law	wife's sister's husband (Indian English)
dada	paternal grandfather (Hindi)
dadi	paternal grandmother (Hindi)
didi	elder sister (Hindi)
ghar-jamai	a man living in his wife's family's home (Hindi)
jija	an elder brother-in-law (Hindi)
joint family	extended family (Indian English)
mama	mother's brother (Hindi)
nana	maternal grandfather (Hindi)
nanad	sister-in-law (Hindi)
nani	maternal grandmother (Hindi)
pati	husband (Hindi)

BEHIND THE VEIL

Maidenly modesty prevails with veils of various descriptions, such as the *pallu*, *hizaab*, *burkha*, *ghoongat*, *dupatta*, *chunni*, and *mekhala chador*, which combine to cover a woman's face, bosom, head, or entire body.

patni	wife (Hindi)
pita-ji	father (Hindi)
puttar	son (Punjabi)
rakhi brother	adopted brother (Hinglish, from Hindi *rakhi*, the sacred thread sisters tie on their brothers' wrists on Raksha Bandhan Day)
saala	wife's brother (Hindi)
saas	mother-in-law (Hindi)
sasur	father-in-law (Hindi)

BIG BROTHER

Most cousins are referred to as *cousin brothers* and *cousin sisters* so that when it comes to actual siblings, the correct usage becomes *real brother* and *real sister*.

IN THE HOME

In villages, alongside traditional huts, sprawling houses with *aangans* (open courtyards) can be found, while *flats* (apartments) in cities are tightly packed and more impersonal. The artefacts of domestic reality have their own language in India:

almirah	a cupboard (Portuguese)
barsaati	a room illegally constructed on a terrace (Hindi for 'rainy')
bhavan	a building (Hindi)
bistar	a bed (Hindi)
body bath	a wash without washing the hair
chabootra	a platform inside a house (Hindi)
charpoy	a bed (Urdu)
chawl	a locality where poorer families live sharing common space and latrines (Hindi)
chimney	a kitchen ventilator
choolha	a mud stove (Hindi)
colony	a residential community, often gated
compound	the privately owned area around a dwelling
duplex	a double-storey dwelling

farmhouse	a type of sprawling house in the suburbs owned byt the rich
gaslet	kerosene (Hindi)
inner courtyard	open areas within old homesteads where women congregate
kuti	a cottage (Hindi, from Sanskrit)
mandi	a marketplace (Hindi)
municipality dump	a designated garbage dump
pandal	a covered outdoor area (Hindi)
quarters	flats for government servants
ration card	the card issued for buying essential commodities at subsidised prices through a state-run Public Distribution System
shamiana	a colourful tent or awning popular for outdoor festivities such as weddings (Hindi)
sloping roofs	old red-tiled roofs
tandoor	a clay oven for cooking meat or vegetables on a spit (Hindi)
teak	a type of tropical wood, mainly from Kerala and Tamil Nadu, prized for making furniture
terrace house	a home with a terrace

HOUSE-WARMINGS

A typical Indian house-warming consists of the *puja* (prayers) and the ritual of letting milk boil over before moving in. These rituals should occur during a *muhurat* (auspicious moment) picked out by the family *pundit* (Hindu religious figure) or a *padri* (Christian priest).

LOVE & MARRIAGE

Though the internet is breaking down boundaries for bashful *Majnus* and *Lailas* (legendary lovers, like Romeo and Juliet) by creating a platform to court in cyberspace, the average Indian woos and coos rather discreetly. University campuses ring with painful cries of *maar daala* (Hindi for 'I've been killed', meaning 'wooed') and *kambakht ishq* (Urdu for 'darn love') as teenagers give *taali* (high-fives) and enjoy *bindaas* (cool) lives. City life does throw up more and more unmarried couples now who are living together almost as *Mr and Mrs* and call themselves *married-sharried* to lower their *house-owner's* (landlord's) eyebrows. In parks and bars, a man and a woman, whether an unmarried couple or just friends, now say they are simply *yaar* (pals) rather than hastily introducing each other as *cousins*, which makes it *all right*, morally speaking, whereas courting in public was, and in many parts of India still is, taboo. English is definitely the cool lingo for love and also for those who are anti-ageing as the language of modernism and *jawani* (youth).

An infatuated fellow is a *Heer*, a *Majnu*, a *Devdas* (all legendary lovelorn heroes) or even a *Romeo*. Infatuated people can also be described as *lattoo* (Hindi for 'spinning like a top'), *diwana* (Hindi for 'crazy') or *aashiq* (Urdu for 'a lover'). Men are liable to come wooing with terms like *haseena* (beauty), *jaaneman* (darling) and *jigar-ka-tukda* (piece of heart), while women need only bask in the compliments, or deflect those which are unwanted.

GETTING OFF

There are a few red herrings to watch out for in the dating arena. To *hit on someone* (American English for 'flirt with someone') in Indian English means to 'beat someone physically' while *coming on* (American English for 'serious flirting') in Indian English is the arrival of someone into, say, a room and to *get off* (American English for 'enjoy') is to take leave from work.

As *katti* (falling out) and *batti* (making up) goes on between friends, matters of the *dil* (heart) are sorted out at college *socials* (gatherings) or at office *coolers* (water coolers). *He's after me* is a breathless translation of the Hindi phrase *peechhe pada hai*. Clean-shaven Romeos are sometimes dismissed as *chikna* (literally 'smooth skin'). 'Give me an intro,' a besotted teenager may beseech the beloved's best *dost* (friend). Meanwhile guys who are *cats* are so cool, the ladies to come running.

To youngsters in the New Age cafés and traditional *dhabas* (roadside restaurants), English is a mating language, which goes well with their gelled hair and frayed jeans. It's *cool*, *cat* and *hep*, not to mention *hot* and *happening* to intersperse your speech with English, Hindi and a peppering of your mother-tongue – whether it be Telugu, Oriya or something else altogether.

Here are some extra words of love to look out for:

Adam basher	a budding feminist
Eve teaser	a molester of women
ishq	love (Urdu)
mohabbat	love (Urdu)
pyaar	love (Hindi)
line maroing	flirting (Hinglish, from Hindi *maro* 'to hit')
patao	to woo (Hindi)
pile-on	someone who *piles on* (joins in uninvited or unasked)
roadside Romeo	a lecherous bystander
soft corner	a crush or infatuation

MATTERS OF THE HEART

The word for 'heart' in Hindi is *dil* and the cardiac organ is used in many phrases as Indians speak *dil se* (from the heart):

dil hi dil mein	heart of hearts (Hindi)
dil ki baat	from the inner recess of the heart (the real desire) (Hindi)
dil-o-dimag	heart and head (Hindi)
dil nahi karta	I don't feel like it, literally 'the heart does not want it' (Hindi)
dil-vil	heart-shmart, a nonsense rhyme (Hindi)

Home & family

63

THE KAMASUTRA

The *Kamasutra* is an ancient Hindu treatise which includes rules for sexual and sensual love and marriage. Compiled by Mallanaga Vatsyayana in the time of the Gupta Empire more than 1500 years ago, it has recently been popularised in the West by marital therapists and psychologists. The elements of the Sanskrit word are *kama* 'love' and *sutra* 'thread'.

The successful marrying-off of sons and daughters is a big deal to many Indian families. A marriageable girl's parents worry until her hands are dyed *peele* ('yellow', from the Hindi saying *haath peele karana* 'make hands yellow', a euphemism for marriage as the bride's hands are decorated with henna).

Matrimonial advertisements frequently call for *virgin brides*, while divorced men, widowers and older bachelors might seek *issueless divorcees* and even *innocent divorcees* to signify the highly prized *purity*. However, as more and more youngsters opt out of *arranged marriages* for *love marriages*, and divorce statistics steadily spiral upwards, such advertisements may soon be wasted.

In addition to *love marriages* and *arranged marriages*, there are also *love-cum-arranged marriages* where spouses are either introduced by their parents and the introduction is followed by a longish engagement period or the couple meets independently with both families subsequently accepting the match if a *suitable boy/girl* (a good catch) is involved.

Another reality of Indian matchmaking is *marriage brokers*, whose job it is to match eligible men with suitable women. *Marriage bureaus* are commercial matchmaking firms. *Girl-seeing* (also known as *bride-showing*) is when the groom's family visit the prospective bride at her home. A *dowry* is the money given to the groom's family at wedding time, a *register marriage* or *court marriage* indicates a non-religious marriage while a *mixed marriage* is an inter-caste marriage.

Here are some more expressions regarding marriage in India:

baraat	the groom's party on its way to the bride's house (Hindi)
bride burning	the allegation of bumping off a bride for lack of dowry payments
Ladies Sangeet	a bride's pre-wedding ritual with women singing playing the *dholki* (lap drum)
marriage season	October to April is considered the most auspicious time to tie the knot
matrimonials	newspaper ads scouting for brides or grooms
nikaah	a Muslim wedding ceremony (Urdu)
sagai	an engagement (Hindi)
settle down	to marry
shaadi	nuptials (Hindi)
vivah	marriage (Hindi)
would-be	a fiancé(e)

MOONSTRUCK

The moon (*chand* in Hindi) plays a great role in India with most festivals decided on its moods and whims. The face of a beloved, typically a woman, is likened to a full-moon or she is described as *chand ka tukda* (a piece of the moon) or plain *chandni* (moonlight). *I'll get you the moon*, is a common extravagant promise to the beloved, who's also told she is *his moon* or that 'a moonless night denotes the moon's embarrassment to show itself in the presence of his beloved's beauty!' Lullabies refer to *chandamama*, turning the moon into a maternal uncle. The phases of the moon are described as *poornima*, *ardha-poornima*, and *amavas* (full moon, half moon, and no moon respectively)

Education

As the official second language after Hindi and the number one language for business, the ability to speak standard English is indicative of a good education, not to mention ambition. It's often said that those who have university degrees but little fluency in standard English can't really be considered educated. Somewhat bizarrely, errors in one's mother tongue are more likely to be condoned than lapses in English grammar. Indians famously pride themselves on being able to speak the queen's English. This attitude was brilliantly parodied in the hit British TV comedy *The Kumars at No 42*, which starred Sanjeev Bhaskar as a talk-show host who thought he had 'the perfect blend of Indian flavour and English refinement'.

With close to a million teachers and 140 million students – from *first division* (straight-A) students to those who get *anda* (zero, from the Hindi for 'egg') – everyone agrees that education – *primary*, *higher secondary* and *specialised* – is of the highest importance. Here is some school vocabulary in case you find yourself hanging round the bike sheds:

canteen	a favourite hangout for college students where tea and snacks are available (Indian English)
compass box	a pencil case (Indian English)
fuchchas	freshers in a college (Indian English)
Madam/Miss	address term for female teachers (Indian English)
madrasa	an Islamic religious school (Urdu)
paper leak	when test papers are deliberately leaked for monetary gain (Indian English)
ragging	the tormenting of freshmen by senior students (Indian English)
scale	ruler (Indian English)
slate	piece of black slate, used to write on with chalk (Indian English)
Sir	address term for male teachers (Indian English)

Literature

With a literary tradition spanning thousands of years, India boasts no shortage of great works. However, despite 200 years of British colonial rule, only scant literature was produced in English before Independence (1947). The most noteworthy pre-Independence texts from an English perspective come from a handful of sacred writings and a few choice authors.

The tradition of Indians writing in English dates back to 1830. The charge was led by *Kashiprasad Ghosh* (1809–1873) (considered the first Indian poet to write in English) and *Sochee Chunder Dutt* (ostensibly the first Indian to write fiction in English).

EDUCATIONAL ACRONYMS

Specialised education in prestigious institutes is a dream come true for most Indian students, with many taking extra tutorials after school or college to qualify. Students vie for positions at the well-known learning centres, such as those listed below.

BITS	Birla Institute of Technology and Science, Pilani (Rajasthan) and Ranchi (Bihar)
CAT	Common Admission Test (an entrance test for the management programmes of the Indian Institute of Management)
DU	Delhi University
JEE	Joint Entrance Exam (a fiercely competitive college entrance exam)
JNU	Jawaharlal Nehru University, New Delhi
IIMC	Indian Institute of Mass Communication, New Delhi
IIT	Indian Institute of Technology
IIM	Indian Institute of Management
NID	National Institute of Design, Ahmedabad
NIFT	National Institute of Fashion Technology

Indian English literature exploded after Independence. While many writers celebrated the departure of British rule by writing in their own regional languages, English was nonetheless in India to stay. Despite ongoing protests by Indians who regard English as an imperialist relic forced upon the subcontinent by outsiders and embraced only by Anglo-wannabes, many believe that Indian English literature is of vast importance on the world stage.

In his introduction to *The Vintage Book of Indian Writing*, published in 1997), Booker Prize–winning author **Salman Rushdie** (b 1947) underscores the vital role literature written in English played in postindependence Indian culture. Rushdie claims that the new Indo-Anglian literature overshadows any other Indian writing since WWII. Of course, with world-famous (and notorious) works such as the monumental *Midnight's Children* (1981) and *The Satanic Verses* (1988) to his name, Rushdie can claim no small part in this contribution.

Whatever the case, India's contribution to English literature is formidable. After the USA and the UK, India is the third largest producer of books published in English. Most publications in English in India contain stylistic influences distilled from regional languages.

Post-Independence Indian literature revolves around a few central themes – what it means to be Indian, how the land's history and spiritual nature can be reconciled with a modern mindset, and whether India is on the threshold of greatness or in an advanced state of decay.

RK Narayan (1906–2001) explores these questions by creating the fictional town of Malgudi, where progress is juxtaposed with tradition in often humorous settings. In his short story *Fellow-Feeling* (1959), a train bully mocks a Brahmin passenger, accusing him of snobbery. Showing that he can walk th ewalk, the Brahmin proceeds to trick and publicly humiliate the bully. It's a commentary on changing values and declining respect (previously the Brahmin would have been sacrosanct), combined with a wits-is-better-than-bluster lesson.

The famous film director **Satyajit Ray** (1921–1992) neatly embodies the blurring of the spiritual and the mundane in his short story *Big Bill* (1987), in which the central character Tulsi Babu is unimpressed by such lofty things as rainbows and nobility – but is brought to his knees by a great mutton *kebab* at Mansur's.'

ANCIENT AVATARS

Written in Sanskrit roughly two millennia ago, the two great Hindu epics – the *Ramayana* and the *Mahabharata* – have impacted almost all writing emanating from the subcontinent, and references to their characters and plots abound.

The *Ramayana*, which is Sanskrit for 'Rama's journey', is the tale of the noble prince Rama, who is an *avatar* (physical manifestation) of the god Vishnu, his wife Sita and his half-brother Lakshmana. Modern Hindus view Rama and Sita as exemplars of dedication to *dharma* (one's duty in life). Both endure significant hardship and personal loss that results from doing their duty. Other themes explored in the *Ramayana* are brotherhood, friendship and the nature of promises.

The *Mahabharata* (loosely translated as 'Great India') is essentially a tale of the struggle for the kingdom of India between two family factions. Central to the text is the story of **Krishna**, a cowherd *avatar* of Lord Vishnu. Convoluted and protracted, the epic twists and turns and eventually ends with the passing of the age of nobility into the current age, in which humankind descends away from the heavenly and towards the base and immoral.

In more recent times, a subtle split between North Indian and South Indian literature has begun revealing itself. Much North Indian literature weaves Hindustani terms through its narratives, rendering the vernacular an integral part of the text, while South Indian authors use English to paint lush landscapes and complex patterns.

In her most famous novel, *In Custody* (1984), Delhi native **Anita Desai** (b 1937) writes of a poet-academic whose love for the 'decaying language' of Urdu consumes his days and nights. The work of **Rohinton Mistry** (b 1952), a Parsi (Zoroastrian) author, is peppered with Hindi, Bombay-Hindi and Hinglish terms, such as when a villager grabs another by the scruff of the neck and demands **Arre choosya?** (OK, choose already!) in *The Collectors* (1985). In his sweeping, epic novel *A Suitable Boy* (1993), **Vikram Seth** (b 1952) tells of a **khatri** (high-caste) mother who rails against her daughter for choosing a Muslim man. The mother invokes the Urdu/Arabic term for divorce, telling her daughter that a year after marrying her, her husband will divorce her by saying 'Talaq talaq talaq'.

Meanwhile, in her ground-breaking debut novel *The God of Small Things* (1997), Keralite-Bengali **Arundhati Roy** (b 1961) uses a graceful command of the English language to paint lingering images of the South Indian landscape. She invokes the punchy pacing of the Malayalam language through her rhythm rather than vocabulary.

No discussion of Indian English literature can be complete without mention of **VS Naipaul** (b 1932), a Trinidadian author who journeyed to India to discover his heritage. In works such as *An Area of Darkness* (1964) and *India: A Million Muti-*

nies Now (1990), he expresses a deep pessimism and widespread criticism of Indian culture, lifestyle and direction. Seen as an 'outsider looking in' by many Indians, Naipaul nevertheless captures another side of the Indian condition in his work.

Newspapers & magazines

Print journalism in India, both vernacular and English, has recently undergone startling changes after the advent of new technologies, and newspapers and magazines have multiplied merrily despite the growing number of TV channels. The *Times of India* is the largest-selling English newspaper, with more than 2 million copies sold daily. The other major English newspapers are the *Hindustan Times,* the *Hindu,* the *Indian Express,* the *Deccan Herald,* the *Statesman* and the *Telegraph.*

Newspaper headlines and advertising copy provide examples of Indian English and Hinglish in action:

anticipatory bail denied bail application rejected (Indian English)

bandh total in Valley news headline meaning 'total strike in Kashmir valley' (Hinglish, from Hindi **bandh** 'stop')

chak de phatte 'kick some ass', used in Indian English ads (Punjabi for 'pick up the boards')

needful will be done, says minister news headline meaning that adequate steps will be taken (Indian English)

MASSIVE MEDIA

TV VJs and radio jockeys are merging English with popular usages in other languages to come up with a listener-friendly, seamless form of chat. For instance, the word 'dedicate' is yet to find a suitable replacement in other Indian languages. A Malayalam TV channel will ask its viewers 'whom shall I dedicate this song to?' with all words except 'dedicate' in Malayalam. Here are some essential Indian media players:

AIR	*All-India Radio*, the state-owned radio station
DD	*Doordarshan*, the state-owned TV station
DNA	*Daily News and Analysis*, a newspaper
ET	the *Economic Times*, the country's leading financial newspaper
Express	the *Indian Express*, a newspaper
HT	*Hindustan Times*, New Delhi's leading newspaper
IANS	*Indo-Asian News Service*, a news agency
Mid-Day	the leading afternoon tabloid from Mumbai
Prasar Bharti	Indian Broadcasting, the government body responsible for the state-run TV and radio channels
PTI	*Press Trust of India*, a news agency
Radio Mirchi	a popular FM radio station
TOI	the *Times of India* newspaper
UNI	*United News of India*, a news agency

dharna at dam site 'strike at proposed dam site' (Hinglish)

workers gherao manager 'workers surround manager', from Hindi *'gher'* meaning 'to circle' (Hinglish)

locals make halla about drainage block 'locals make noise about drainage block', from Hindi *'halla'* for 'noise' (Hinglish)

party members on a morcha 'political party members march to protest', from Hindi *'morcha'* meaning 'march by protesters for political reasons' (Hinglish)

Shankaracharya back in mutt newspaper headline meaning that the religious leader Shankaracharya returned to the *mutt* (Hindi for 'monastic order') (Hinglish)

monsoon session of parliament preponed newspaper headline meaning that the parliament session is brought forward due to the monsoon season which starts in June (Indian English)

total tashan used in ads and chat-shows, *tashan* is Punjabi for 'style'

Work & business

India is one of the top five industrialised nations of the world, producing every conceivable industrial item as well as consumer goods. With large cities and urban centres mushrooming, a burgeoning middle class and new working class have emerged with their heads well above the breadline. The language that connects them is Indian English, which is as elastic as the emerging ***East Asian Tiger*** economy it unites, components of which the following terms describe:

BPO Business Process Outsourcing unit, an enterprise, such as a call centre, set up to perform outsourced functions for foreign companies

cottage industry an industry of a traditional nature catering mainly to a local population and depending upon raw materials

derecognise to stop recognising or to blacklist

SSI   a Small Scale Industry, meaning a small business

tiny sector   term referring to businesses smaller than SSIs, but bigger than cottage industries

upgradation   an upgrade

The average middle class Indian male can be found working nine to five in a government office as an **LDC** (lower division clerk) or an **HDC** (higher division clerk). He should make enough to buy a house, see his son settled and to marry off his daughter. He will then consider his duty as a provider done and, upon retirement, will receive a state pension. In contrast, an upper-middle-class man will always aspire to greater wealth. He will send his children to the West for higher studies and will look forward to marrying off his daughter and throwing a wedding reception that lasts a week. The following are some terms which are commonly hear around the office in India:

age-barred   to be ineligible for applying due to age

apply, apply, no reply   a common saying when no response is received to a job application

badli   a temporary worker (Hindi)

bada sahib   a senior boss (Hindi/Urdu)

bonded labourer   an indentured worker

chhota sahib   a junior boss (Hindi/Urdu)

chowkidar   a guard-cum-errand-boy at an office or residential building (Hindi)

chutti   a holiday (Hindi)

dearness allowance   part of an official salary meant to compensate for the prevailing levels of inflation

get off   to take a day of leave

half-day leave   leave work at noon or work only from noon

peon   a messenger or attendant in an office

Regardless of the cultural potpourri in India and a conscious yearning to amalgamate the strands of the past and the present, crisp and chaste English is still seen as a trophy language. Employers cock their ears to sift through your accent at job interviews, *matrimonial ads* scout for convent-educated, English-speaking brides, and students desirous of *MNC* (multinational corporation) posts or foreign assignments eschew speaking any language except English to gain an upmarket-style fluency.

The snob value attached to impeccable spoken English, called *unaccented* or *accentless*, is still strong in some circles. Strong regional Indian accents are looked down on and being told by someone that they 'can't guess your state from your accent' is a wonderful compliment. The urban phenomenon of call centres has, of course, precipitated a veritable landslide of people aspiring to speak varieties of English unblemished by their mother tongue. Workers are trained in English accents by *accent trainers* based in the big cities. The idea is to enable students to converse seamlessly and on an equal footing with clients from Alaska to Adelaide. Even people from small towns, where election rhetoric has failed to translate into electricity and tap water, enrol in

GRASS ROOTS

The odd formality of Indian English in official correspondence is a hangover from the British imperial past. 'We sincerely hope that you will do the needful at your earliest possible convenience' is a fairly typical turn of phrase in an official letter. Such formality is, however, counterbalanced in the actual workplace. A boss would think nothing of dressing down a lazy employee with the accusatory phrase 'What are you doing, cutting grass?' or even 'What are you doing, chasing flies?' The colloquial expression *cutting grass* harks back to India's past where it was the role of servants to cut grass. The menial labour of servants is nowadays regarded as worthless, giving rise to the derogatory meaning of the modern phrase.

spoken English classes to mask any embarrassing regional implications in pronunciation.

The future of English was only cemented further with the arrival of internet. With over 15 fonts necessary to use the main Indian languages on a keyboard (although with new technologies, this is becoming easier by the second), English became a simpler option. Computers spelt the doom of British English in India, as spell checkers and idioms brought on American English. Despite this it would be incorrect to say that India has given up on British English. The queen's English remains the model way of speaking English. While American English stands for youth and change, British English stands guard over the 'right' path to English in its entirety.

Meanwhile, *NRIs* (Non-Resident Indians) are busy pollinating India with a multitude of English accents on their back-to-roots holidays or by relocating to the 'motherland'.

Politics

In politics, English forms a much-needed bridge, given the fact that politicians come from different states and have different native languages. When the *Constitution of India* was framed in 1950, English was recognised as the authoritative legislative and judicial language for a period of 15 years, to be then replaced by Hindi. However, the popularity of English has ensured its immortality with no date being set for its replacement by Hindi, the main colloquial organ of the country.

Here are a few terms related to politics in India:

activist	a protestor
bandh	a strike (Hindi)
Bharat Mata	Mother India
booth capturing	cheating by political parties at the voting booth by forcing voters to vote for a particular candidate
curfew	a police clampdown in a city following unrest
disproportionate assets	assets bought with unaccounted-for money, disproportionate to one's income
CM	the Chief Minister (of a state)
FM	the Finance Minister
horse trading	the illegal buying and selling of MLAs (Members of the Legislative Assembly) and MPs to make up numbers in electoral battles
HRD	Human Resource Development
indefinite fast	a hunger strike for a demand
Lok Sabha	the lower house of parliament (Hindi)
majlis	the parliament (Urdu)
mantri	a political minister (Hindi)
mantralaya	ministerial offices (Hindi)
MEA	the Ministry of External Affairs
MLA	a Member of the Legislative Assembly
morcha	a protest rally (Hindi)
MP	a Member of Parliament
mulk	country, place of origin (Urdu)
naxalites	members of a breakaway group of the *Communist Party of India,* they believe in social reform through violent revolution
PoK	Pakistan-occupied Kashmir
panchayat	a village-level administration unit (Hindi)
parishad	a unit (Hindi)

Politics

77

pradesh	a state (Hindi)
president's rule	when no party has a clear majority in a state legislature, *president's rule* is imposed
Rashtrapati Bhavan	the presidential residence in New Delhi (Hindi)
Rajya Sabha	the upper house of parliament, (Hindi)
sena	the army (Hindi)
taluka	a sub-section of a district (Urdu)
watan	homeland (Urdu, from Farsi)
zilla	a zone (district) (Urdu)
zindabad	'long live' (a victory cry or blessing), (Urdu)

Here is some political vocabulary from important events in modern Indian political life:

Green Revolution the introduction of high-yielding varieties of rice, wheat etc into Indian farms in the late '60s

Independence freedom from British rule obtained on 15 August 1947

Satyameva Jayate The Truth Always Wins, a motto of the Indian justice system (Sanskrit)

Anti-Sikh Riots the anti-Sikh riots which followed in the wake of former prime minister Indira Gandhi's assassination by her Sikh bodyguards in 1984

ON THE BLOCK

In Delhi the administrative organs of the country's government are housed in imposing imperial edifices known as **North Block** and **South Block**. **North Block** houses the offices of the Home and Finance ministries while **South Block** houses Defence, External Affairs and the Prime Minister's Office (**PMO**).

THE UNDERWORLD

India's criminal underbelly has been depicted in a number of films such as *Don, Satya (Truth), Company, Godmother, Sarkar* and *D*. The Indian underworld and the fight of the police against it has also contributed a number of terms to Indian English:

absconding	the escape of a criminal (Indian English)
anticipatory bail	bail paid in anticipation of accusation, before being accused formally. Then, if formally charged, the accused is let off on bail. (Indian English)
bhai	a member of the underworld (Hindi for 'brother')
bhai-log	the underworld mafia (Hindi for 'brother people')
black money	money obtained through illegal channels (Indian English)
chai-paani	slang for a bribe (Hindi for 'tea-water')
charge sheet	a formal case sheet where the charges are spelt out (Indian English)
gun battle	the exchange of gunfire (Indian English)
police chowki	a police station (Hinglish, from Hindi *chowki* 'platform')
don	an underworld boss (Indian English, from Italian)
hawala	illegal monetary transactions across borders (Hindi)
speed money	a bribe (Indian English)
supari	an advance paid for bumping someone off (Hindi for 'betel nut')
undertrial	the accused undergoing formal trial, eg *the undertrial fainted in court* (Indian English)

Politics

Emergency   the political clampdown by then prime minister Indira Gandhi in the mid-'70s that lasted 19 nightmarish months

Godhra Riots   at least 1000 people were killed in the 2002 carnage that broke out following the burning of 58 Hindu activists in a train at Godhra on 27 February 2002

garibi hatao   a Hindi political slogan meaning 'remove poverty', coined by the late prime minister Indira Gandhi in the '70s

Operation Blue Star   the controversial 1984 operation to evict Sikh militant separatists from the Golden Temple in Amritsar, Punjab, by sending in the army

Quit India   the 1942 movement of organised civil disobedience aiming for the immediate independence of India from British rule

salt satyagraha   a march to protest against British salt tax in colonial India undertaken by Mahatma Gandhi to the Dandi seashore in Gujarat where the protesters made their own salt (Hinglish, English *salt* plus **satyagraha,** the name given to the nonviolent resistance movement popularised by Gandhi, from Hindi *satya* 'truth' *agraha* 'desire')

Vande Mataram   a song composed by Bankimchandra Chattopadhyay, which was once the rallying cry for freedom from British rule (literally 'Salute to the Motherland' in Sanskrit)

White Revolution   the boom in milk supplies, thanks to a successful cooperative movement initiated in Anand, Gujarat, by Dr V Kurien in the '60s

Spirituality

If India were any more spiritual, the whole subcontinent would begin levitating – it's the birthplace of scores of religions, not to mention countless relaxation and meditation techniques.

It is estimated that around 80 per cent of the population are practicing Hindus. The other major religions are Islam, Christianity, Sikhism, and Buddhism. Of course, in a nation of over a billion people, even the minor religions, such as Zoroastrianism and Judaism, still have larger followings than some countries have citizens.

HINDUISM

Dharma (the path of truth and duty) and *karma* (fate) mark a Hindu's *jeevan* (life) as *puja* (rituals) are performed to appease not just the gods but also one's forefathers whose heavenly *atmas* (souls) could be jeopardised by not keeping *vrat* (fasting) as the Hindu calendar demands. Belief in reincarnation (*punar-janam* in Hindi/Sanskrit) or the resonant *Om*, symbolising the beginning and end of the universe, or even the religious chants that come from the *Vedas* (Hindu scriptures), is perfectly in sync with feeding milk to snakes to please Lord Shiva or throwing wheat balls to fishes to promote fertility. Meditation is just one of the *mantras* (instruments of thought) up a Hindu's sleeve on his or her path to spiritual *moksha* (enlightenment). What cannot be controlled is down to *kismet* (Urdu for 'fate'). Some terms related to the Hindu faith include the following:

aarti   the ritual of moving a small flame held in the right hand in a circular motion before an idol (Hindi)

ardha-narishwar   a fusion of Shiva and Shakti/Parvati, represented by a half man and half woman image (Sanskrit)

acharya   teacher of philosophy and spirituality (Hindi)

ashram   a religious retreat or community where a Hindu holy man resides with his followers (Hindi)

HOLY DAYS

As a country with many religions, India has a lot of religious festivals and holy days. The dates given in brackets below are from the Hindu or Muslim calendars as opposed to the Gregorian (Christian) calendar, used in the West. Just like Easter, many of the dates depend on the cycles of the moon.

Muharram   10 Muharram (January)
Also called the Day of Ashura, Muharram commemorates the martyrdom of Hazrat Imam Hussain, the grandson of Prophet Mohammad. Muharram is also the name of the first month of the Muslim calendar, which is roughly equivalent to January.

Maha Shivratri   Phalguna (March)
Hindus perform *puja* (worship) to Lord Shiva by fasting on this day. This festival takes place on the eve of the new moon in Phalguna (roughly March) in the Hindu Calendar.

Ram Navami   9 Chaitra (April)
The birth anniversary of the Hindu god Lord Rama, remembered for his righteous reign, falls on the 9th day of the Hindu month of Chaitra (roughly equivalent to April).

Buddha Purnima   Vaisakh (May)
Also called *Buddha Jayanti*, the birth anniversary of Buddha is celebrated on this day, the full moon in the Hindu month of Vaisakh (roughly May). His achievement of enlightenment is celebrated on the same date.

Janmashtami   Sravana (August)
The birth anniversary of Lord Krishna is celebrated on the 8th day of the waning moon in Sravana (roughly August).

Dussehra   Ashwin (October)
Also known as *Navratri*, it is based on the epic story of the *Ramayana*, signifying the triumph of good over evil. Dussehra is celebrated all over India for the killing of the evil King Ravana by Lord Ram of Ayodhya. In Bengal it is observed as *Durga Puja*. Dussehra lasts for 10 days.

Idu'l Fitr   1 Syawal (November)
This is celebrated to mark the end of Ramzan (Ramadan), the Muslim month of fasting.

Guru Nanak Jayanti   Kartik (November)
The Sikh community celebrates the birth anniversary of its founder Guru Nanak on the full moon of the Hindu month Kartik (approximately October or November).

Id-ul Zuha   10 Zil Hijja (December)
Also known as *Eid al-Adha* or *Bakr-id*, Id-ul Zuha is celebrated in memory of Ibrahim's (Abraham's) faith in god. Ibrahim was willing to unquestioningly sacrifice his son Ismail (Isaac) as god asked. Id-ul Zuha falls on the 10th day of Muslim month Zil Hijja, which is roughly equivalent to December.

atma   the soul (Hindi)

bhagwan   a god (Hindi)

bhakti   devotion to a god (Hindi)

brahmin   an upper-caste Hindu (Hindi/Sanskrit)

camphor   an aromatic substance obtained from the camphor tree burned for the auspicious ambience it imparts (Indian English, from Arabic via Latin)

devi   any goddess (Hindi)

daan   charity (Hindi)

darshan   a divine vision or sighting (Hindi)

devaswom   temple board of trustees in the South (Sanskrit)

godman   spiritual leader with a following; increasingly the term carries a whiff of charlatanism

kanwaria devotees who walk barefoot to fetch Ganges water to pour over Lord Shiva's idol (Hindi)

pran the life-sustaining force of both the individual and the universe (Hindi)

pranam a religious salute (Hindi)

kundalini inner strength based in the spine (Sanskrit)

gurukul students boarding with a *guru* (Hindi)

havan Hindi for 'fire sacrifice', a *havan* is a prayer done to *Agni*, the god of fire, seeking divine intervention

jaadu-tona magical hocus-pocus (Hindi)

janeyu a holy thread worn across the chest by Hindus (Hindi)

jantar-mantar aids/mantra for meditation (Hindi)

lingam the holy sign of Lord Shiva (Sanskrit)

mantra a divine chant, such as the well-known *Gayatri Mantra* (Hindi)

KRISHNA

Krishna (also known as the *Blue Lord*) is the most popular Hindu god. Depicted as a flute-playing shepherd sporting a peacock feather in his crown, he also happens to be an incarnation of Lord Vishnu and has many other names including Govardhan, Keshav, Gopal, Kishen, Kanhaiya, Hari, Shyam, Govind and Giridhar. In the *Mahabharata*, his advice to Pandava Prince Arjuna, who is reluctant to confront his relatives and teachers on the battlefield, constitutes the epic *Bhagvad Gita,* a timeless discourse on life and duty.

muni a monk who has taken a vow of silence, usually refers to a Jain ascetic (Hindi)

pandal a stage for idols (Hindi)

parikrama a Hindu, Sikh, Buddhist and Jain rite of walking around the object of worship (Hindi)

prabhu a Hindu lord (Hindi)

rangoli an auspicious drawing outside the front door of a house (Hindi)

rath a horse-drawn chariot, sometimes harnessed for religious or political pageants (Hindi)

rishi Hindu religious teachers of yore who dwelt in forests and mountains (Hindi)

rudraksh holy beads (Hindi)

sant an honorific title for spiritual leaders by devotees (Hindi)

sanyasi a Hindu who has renounced all ties except to god (Hindi)

THE HINDU PANTHEON

According to Hindu mythology, *Brahma* is the Creator of the Universe, *Vishnu* the Preserver and *Shiva* the Destroyer. Together they form the divine ruling trinity. Krishna is another popular god, see boxed text p84. Others in the divine cast include:

Hanuman the monkey god, who signifies loyalty and celibacy, from the epic Ramayana (see boxed text p70)

Kama the god of love and desire, a divine Cupid

Lakshmi the goddess of wealth

Saraswati the goddess of learning

Shanidev the planet Saturn, which bodes bad luck, and is to be warded off with special prayers

Yama the god of death

shloka poems from Sanskrit scriptures which are chanted during Hindu rites like marriages and funerals (Sanskrit)

shubh auspicious (Hindi)

swami a title of respect for a Hindu holy man or teacher (Hindi)

Tantra a system of philosophy based on sacred texts written between the 7th and 17th centuries (Sanskrit)

third eye the sixth *chakra* (centre of life-force energy), located between the eyebrows; a symbol of enlightenment (Indian English)

Tower of Silence a Parsi funeral site where the deceased are left outside for the vultures to eat (Indian English)

trishul Lord Shiva's trident (Hindi)

vrat Hindu fasts (Hindi)

yagna prolonged prayers, involving *havan* (fire worship) (Sanskrit)

HOLY COW!

Hindus venerate the cow as *gou mata* or 'cow-mother'. Hence you will seldom find beef on the menu. You will often find cows sitting bang in the middle of the road, blocking traffic, ignoring the tooting horns as they chew languidly on *chapattis* (flat breads) offered by *bhakts* (the devout). Lord Krishna, the bodily incarnation of the supreme god Vishnu, was a cowherd and is usually depicted dreamily playing the flute while chilling with his bovine buddies.

ISLAM

After Hinduism, Islam is India's biggest religion. The country is also home to the second largest Muslim population in the world. Here are some important terms relating to Islam:

Allah	god (Arabic)
azan	a call to prayer (Urdu)
dargah	a holy shrine (Urdu)
Haj	a pilgrimage to Mecca and Medina (Arabic)
imam	leader in Islamic theology (Urdu, from Arabic)
juma	Friday prayers (Urdu)
khuda	god (Urdu)
Koran	Muslim scripture (Arabic)
insha-Allah	god-willing (Arabic)
madrasa	a religious school (Arabic)
moulvi	a priest (Urdu)
muezzin	the person who calls people to prayers (Arabic)
mujahideen	a freedom fighter (Arabic)
Musalman	a Muslim (Urdu)
namaaz	prayers (Urdu)
roza	a strict dawn-to-dusk fast during *Ramzan* (Ramadan) (Urdu)
Shia	one of the two main branches of Islam, along with *Sunni* (Arabic)
Sunni	the other main branch of Islam, along with *Shia* (Arabic)
Sufi	Sufism is a mystical dimension of Islam with likely roots in early Hinduism (Urdu)
subhan-Allah	a refrain meaning 'God is glorious' (Arabic)
Wakf	a Muslim trust board (Urdu)
zakat	a charity (Arabic)

SIKHISM

The five *k*'s are central to the Sikh faith. These items are worn by followers as a demonstration of solidarity and out of respect for their teacher Guru Gobind Singh. They are *kesh* (long hair), *kangha* (the ritual comb), *kada* (an iron bracelet signifying the believer's link to the Guru and with fellow believers), *kirpan* (ceremonial dagger, a symbol of dignity and defence of the weak) and *kachchha* (these soldier shorts signify high moral character and control over passion). Other key words in the Sikh vocabulary include:

Waheguru   God (Punjabi)

gurudwara   a Sikh temple (Punjabi)

langar   a *gurudwara* kitchen where food is served free to all who come (Punjabi)

paath   readings from Sikh scriptures (Hindi/Punjabi)

BUDDHISM

Born in the 6th century BC in an area of today's Bihar state, Gautama Siddhartha was no ordinary Hindu prince. Leaving his family, the palace and every luxury behind, he wandered around, living on alms, seeking the meaning of life. After rigorous and long meditation under a *peepul* tree, he gained enlightenment and became the Buddha (the enlightened one). The Buddha's teachings have given rise to the religion of Buddhism, which is noticeably bereft of deities and rituals. The three divisions are Theravada, East Asian Buddhism and Tibetan Buddhism.

bhikshu   Buddhist monk who lives on alms (Sanskrit)

bodha vriksha   the *peepul* tree or Bodhi Tree under which Buddha gained enlightenment (Sanskrit, literally 'enlightenment tree')

Buddha   commonly used to refer to Gautama Siddhartha, the prince and historical founder of Buddhism

Buddham saranam gachami   a funeral song (Sanskrit, literally 'I go to the Buddha for refuge')

Dalai Lama   the spiritual leader of Tibetan Buddhism

nirvana   Sanskrit for spiritual liberation

Yatra (travel) entails being on the move. In the cities, prepare for *bheed* (bustling crowds), insane traffic and the inevitable tooting horns. The rubber hooters preferred by *cycle-rickshaws* are dubbed *pom-pom*, while the shrill whistle-type horns pumped incessantly by *auto-rickshaw* drivers are known as *pee-pee*. Roads are chaotic. The side of the highway is a public latrine for pedestrians who also double as tourist guides: they are usually more than happy to point out popular landmarks with their free hands.

As with any journey, your first mission is always to plan the *kaise* (hows), *kahan* (wheres) and even *kyon* (whys) of the excursion. Exploring every *kona-kona* (nook and cranny) of this magnificent country takes some doing but it's worth it if only for the sake of meeting the extraordinary *Hindustani log* (Indian people).

Before setting off, take a moment to set your watch to *IST* (Indian Standard Time), which you'll notice often equates to 'terribly late'. To achieve *nirvana* you must first abandon your schedule. Doing so will make you feel lighter and more agile, so you can athletically dodge *three-wheelers* (auto-rickshaws) emblazoned with monikers such as *Munnu di gaddi* (Punjabi for 'this is Munnu's vehicle') or, in the south, leap out the way of buses baptised *Joseph* or *Rani*. Whenever boarding your chosen mode of transport, whether this is a jeep that has never known the meaning of roadworthy, or a laconic camel ready to spit in your eye, it's important that you embrace the inevitable *starting trouble* as your driver waves a hand in the universal sign for *nahi* (no) and heads off in search of a mechanic or a vet.

Somewhere along your epic travelling adventure the following words and phrases will undoubtedly cross your path:

back up   to reverse (Indian English)

backwaters   the meandering network of rivers and lakes connected by canals in the southern state of Kerala (Indian English)

boutique   a wayside shop selling clothes (Indian English)

Brahmin hotel   a vegetarian restaurant (Indian English, *Brahmin* is an upper-caste Hindu)

charpoy   a crude bed consisting of string across a wooden frame (from Hindi *char* 'four' and *pai* 'legs')

circuit house   a high quality lodging for government staff at a district headquarters (Indian English)

cut   a break in the concrete divider running along the middle of all wide roads to enable motorists to do a U-turn (Indian English)

dak bungalow   a temporary residence for travelling government staff (Hinglish, from Hindi *dak* 'postal service')

dharamshala   cheap lodgings for Hindu pilgrims at religious centres. Not to be confused with the town in northern India of the same name that houses the exiled Tibetan government and the Dalai Lama. (Hindi, from Sanskrit *dharma* 'religion' and *sala* 'abode'.)

fooding and lodging   food and lodging available (Indian English)

foot overbridge   a bridge for pedestrians to cross over railway tracks, roads, etc (Indian English)

footpath pavement (in British English), sidewalk (in American English) (Indian English)

forest bungalow a government lodge for travellers in forest areas (Indian English)

hill station a high-altitude village or resort, providing a cool and green holiday escape (Indian English)

musafirkhana lodgings for Muslim travellers (from Urdu *musafir* 'traveller' and *khana* 'place')

out of station out of town, away from home (Indian English)

parlour a beauty parlour (Indian English)

rail roko a blockade of trains as a form of political or social protest (Hinglish, from Hindi *roko* 'stop')

rest-house a lodge for government employees travelling on official business (Indian English)

road roko a blockade of road traffic (Hinglish, from Hindi *roko* 'stop')

speed-breaker ahead watch out for speed humps (Indian English)

string bed another name for *charpoy* (Indian English)

tirth yatra a Hindu pilgrimage (Hindi)

Udupi restaurant a vegetarian hotel serving primarily South Indian snacks (Indian English, Udupi is a place name)

DRIVING

The saying goes that, if you can *chalao a gaadi* ('drive a vehicle', from Hindi *chalao* 'drive, move or walk' and *gaadi* 'vehicle') in India, then you can drive anywhere on earth. Any bad drivers in India will find themselves the subject of *gaalis* (curses). Manoeuvring through constant rush-hour traffic is as difficult as it looks. In Delhi, signs next to the traffic lights warn you *Don't Take Green for Granted*. The temptation to believe that a green light means 'all clear' is best avoided, as traffic rules are regularly flouted. Road rage is common on metro roadways, where complete strangers can be seen in heated exchanges. Usually these matters are settled by intervening pedestrians before the traffic police can get a word in edgeways. The opposing sides might then even part on amicable terms and sometimes exchange addresses so they can meet up later.

Strangely, conversation and driving are happy bedfellows in India. You will be amazed at the steering dexterity of cyclists and even drivers of cars and *lorries* (trucks) as they attempt to drive side by side just to carry on a conversation.

In most cases, traffic signs are written in two languages, one being English, eg *Bump Ahead* (speed hump ahead). Incidentally, a lot of driving-related words across India are sourced from British English, which has led to the following Hinglish expressions:

brake maarna   brake (from Hindi *maarna* 'hit')

drive pe chalte hain   let's go for a drive (from Hindi *chalte* 'drive, move or walk')

horn bajana   to honk (from Hindi *bajana* 'play')

steering work nahi karta   the steering's broken (from Hindi *nahi karta* 'not doing')

tyre puncture ho gaya   the tyre's punctured (from Hindi *ho gaya* 'has happened')

HORN OK PLEASE

India's anarchic traffic-choked roads resemble a fairground bumper-car ride. The constant tooting of horns constitutes a language of its own. Careful tooting enables complex driving manoeuvres to be undertaken in relative safety. Different toots signal 'yes' or 'no' answers to a driver's signaled intentions. *Lorries* (trucks) in India almost always have the words *Horn OK Please* painted at the rear in bright letters. It is considered a courtesy for other drivers to announce their presence by tooting at them.

Those who venture out into the bedlam of India's highways will no doubt bump into these Indian English expressions:

accidented   describes a vehicle involved in an accident, eg 'I accidented my car' (Indian English)

Ambassadors   brand name for old (soon to be superceded) bulky cars, plying as taxis or government conveyances

auto; auto-rickshaw a three-wheeled motorised vehicle (Indian English)

bund an embankment (Hindi)

carcade motorcade (Indian English)

circle a roundabout; traffic circle (also called *gol chakri* 'round circle' in Hindi) (Indian English)

CNGs vehicles running on eco-friendly, Compressed Natural Gas (Indian English)

cycle-rickshaws a large tricycle-like vehicle with a buggy behind for carrying passengers (Indian English)

dickey the boot of a car (Indian English)

fatal accident sometimes used to describe serious accidents without casualties (Indian English)

Fiat this brand name has come to mean a type of car from the Italian carmaker, made under licence in India. These cars are now almost obsolete and the word is synonymous with 'slow' or 'old'.

marg the Hindi word for 'road' sometimes used instead of the English version, such as Copernicus Marg and Kasturba Gandhi Marg in Delhi

Maruti a relatively modern brand of small, nuclear-family car

meter a device in cabs and ***auto-rickshaws*** that shows the fare. Say *meter se chalo* ('go by meter' Hinglish) or ***go by meter*** to avoid being over-charged. (Indian English)

THE GOLDEN QUADRILATERAL

The term ***Golden Quadrilateral*** refers to the top-quality highways being built to connect the four largest Indian metropolises – Mumbai, Delhi, Kolkata and Chennai.

NH   national highway (Indian English)

petrol pump   a gas/petrol station (Indian English)

prepaid   the system at airports and major railway stations whereby you can hire a cab or **auto-rickshaw** by paying in advance at a counter manned by traffic police, reducing the chances of being cheated on your fare (Indian English)

RTO   Regional Transport Office, which registers vehicles, issues licences etc (Indian English)

sarani   in Kolkata this word (pronounced 'shaw·raw·ni') is used instead of 'road', so that you'd see Shakespeare Sarani and Lenin Sarani (Bengali)

subway   a pedestrian underpass under a busy road

PUBLIC TRANSPORT

Indian Railways operates one of the world's largest networks of long-distance trains. There are two classes of travel – *first class* and *second class* – further divided into *two-tier* and *three-tier* depending on the number of levels of bunks in the compartment. You may also select between a berth that has *AC/non-AC* (air-conditioned/non-air-conditioned) along with meals, specified as *veg/nonveg* (vegetarian/nonvegetarian).

With India's burgeoning population, buses everywhere bulge with people. Some places in India are better connected by road rather than train, like Agra or Puducheri (formerly called Pondicherry), so that bus travel to such places is more rampant. Most states have both short- and long-distance bus services run by government RTCs (road transport corporations), eg KSRTC (Kerala State Road Transport Corporation).

The list below should help you decode the essential loco-motive vocabulary.

BEST Mumbai state transport buses (Brihanmumbai Electric and Suburban Transport)

bogey a railway carriage (Indian English)

bus adda a terminus for long-distance buses (Hinglish, from Hindi *adda* 'den; depot')

check-post a traffic barrier manned by police officials at which vehicles are stopped and searched (Indian English)

conductor a ticket-seller on a bus (Indian English)

DTC the Delhi Transport Corporation, which runs buses

express/superfast a fast train with few stops (Indian English)

fatfati a noisy and large motorbike or auto-rickshaw (Hindi)

ghoda-gaadi a horse-cart (Hindi)

jonga a wide-bodied four-wheel-drive Jeep-like vehicle (brand name)

locals passenger trains in Mumbai (Indian English)

SPEAKING HINDI

Indians have been very adept at assimilating English words into their vocabularies, but the traffic hasn't all been one way. The English word *dinghy* 'a small boat', for example, comes from the Hindi *dingi* meaning 'little boat' from *dinga* 'boat'.

lorry a truck (Indian English; also British English)

metros the inner-city rail system in Delhi and Kolkata (Indian English)

passenger train slow train which makes frequent stops (Indian English)

rake a line of railway wagons (Indian English)

Rajdhani Express long-distance fast trains run by Indian Railways, which connect Delhi to other important centres (from Hindi *rajdhani* 'capital city')

retiring room a room at a railway station where passengers can rest while in transit (Indian English)

Shatabdi Express the other fast-train service run by Indian Railways (see *Rajdhani Express*), which connects metros other than Delhi to other important centres (from Hindi *shatabdi* 'centenary')

scootie abbreviation for scooter (Indian English)

three-wheeler an auto-rickshaw (Indian English)

two-wheeler a motorbike or scooter (Indian English)

TT a train ticket examiner (conductor) (Indian English)

video coach luxury bus plying between towns, equipped with TV screens playing videos at high volume, which interfere with sleep (Indian English)

WT a traveller without a ticket (Indian English)

On trains you will notice that signs in every coach solemnly inform you that to *Stop Train, Pull Chain*. This invitation is sometimes abused by the *janata* (people) to get the train to make unscheduled stops conveniently close to their chosen destinations. Hence the accompanying *Chain-Pullers Will Be Fined* sign.

HOLIDAYING

If you successfully avoid *machchar* (mosquitoes), *Delhi belly* (diarrhoea), and *dhobi's itch* (a skin irritation from clothes washed at *dhobi-ghats*, which are riverside public laundry places), when you're on *chutti* (vacation), then you'll be in for some serious *mauj-masti* (fun-times). Upon reaching your hotel, however, you may need someone to explain how to operate the *(desert) cooler*, a device that sprays water droplets into a fan and is a cheap alternative to air conditioning.

Locals prefer taking their holidays within these parameters:

purnima   a full-moon night (recommended for Taj Mahal viewing as the monument to love was built with special marble that shines in moonlight)

second Saturday   the second Saturday of every month is a holiday in most educational institutions and government organisations. All other Saturdays are working days.

six-day week   the normal working week. A five-day week is observed only in *MNCs* (multinational corporations) that have a uniform holiday code across the globe, and by some government institutions.

Food

The Hindi language doesn't distinguish between lunch and dinner. Both meals are referred to as *khana* (meal). So, when invited to *stay for khana*, you should be prepared to eat either lunch and dinner. Breakfast is *nashta*, so if you're asked to *come for nashta*, you know what you're in for.

Feeding guests until they're ready to burst is an essential part of Indian hospitality. Even though junk food is rapidly increasing in popularity, a formal visit to any home will entail an elaborately prepared traditional meal – perhaps served on a large fresh banana leaf, in lieu of a plate, in southern India. Upon arrival you might be offered something *garam* (hot) – usually this refers to temperature but it could also relate to spice content – or *thanda* (cold). If you say, *Nahi-nahi* (no, no) or *nothing, please*, your host will insist you *take something* as it is the first time you're visiting their home. If you don't, you will be told that the host has cooked with their *own hands* (a literal translation of the Hindi *apne haathon se banaya hai*). The offerings will continue until you *take something*.

Food used to be cooked on a stove using *gobar gas* (methane gas derived from cow dung) but most people are now using LPG. It may also be baked in a *tandoor* (clay oven), imparting a deliciously smoky aroma. The word *hot* refers not to temperature but to spice quotient. Hot in India is of the tongue-scorcher, tears-in-the-eyes, chilli-red, fiery-as-a-furnace variety. Mild food is dismissed as *pheeka* (bland) or *bina masala* (without spice) or simply *tasteless*. To spice things up there are *garam masala* and *meat masala* – powders or pastes made from a range of spices including black pepper, cinnamon, coriander powder, turmeric, chilli powder, cardamom, cumin seeds, fennel, nutmeg and cloves.

After you have done your best to taste everything on your plate or leaf, your host will still look at you as if mortally wounded and sadly remark *you have eaten nothing* – don't panic, this is simply etiquette. In bygone times only a loud burp by guests to signal they were *stomach-full* would satisfy the hosts. Remember to save room for the mandatory sweet.

Meals are served with pickles, *chutney* (a sweet-and-sour paste of mint or coriander leaves, tamarind, and lime juice), *curds* (yogurt), *pappadam* (crisp fried wafers), *dhal* (lentil stew), seasonal vegetables, regional delicacies and rice or *chapatti* (unleavened bread, also known as *roti* in northern India).

India has a variety of delicious fruits and vegetables, many of which may be somewhat unfamiliar to foreign visitors. Here are a variety of the more unfamiliar words for delights from nature:

bitter gourd	green-coloured bitter vegetable with seeds
cuscus	root of vetiver grass (Arabic)
capsicum	bell peppers
curry leaves	leaves used for seasoning in the south; rarely plucked after sunset for superstitious reasons
drumstick	long green vegetable of the Moringa tree
disco papaya	seedless paw-paw
jackfruit	fleshy yellow tropical fruit with cookable seeds
papita	paw-paw (Hindi)
peepul	a sacred tree, often found in temple courtyards (Hindi)
rose apple	bell-shaped green-and-pink-skinned fruit
snake gourd	a long green fruit which grows on a vine; also called white gourd, or serpent gourd
tapioca	tropical root crop; also called cassava
tulsi	basil, which has holy connotations in India (Hindi)

MANGO MAGIC

Indians regard the mango as the king of fruits. There are over 500 varieties of this luscious fruit for you to sample across the subcontinent. Here is some fruity mango language:

mango showers	March–May premonsoonal showers
mangosteen	a purple-skinned fruit
mango relish	a sweet-and-sour mango preparation
mango trick	a famous Indian magic trick where a seed is shown growing into a small mango tree
Mangola; *Maaza*; *Frooti*	mango-flavoured drinks (all brand names)
The House of Blue Mangoes	a novel by the Indian-born writer David Davidar

SNACKS

Not only are Indians fond of elaborate meals, they don't mind indulging in a bit of *tiffin* (snacks). The word *tiffin* has been extended to encompass anything, including full meals, that is carted around in a *dabba* (a metal box with numerous sealed compartments). Mumbai is *tiffin* obsessed: the Mumbai Tiffin Box Suppliers Association has over 4500 members who supply millions of lunches each year to the city's office workers.

Popular street snacks consist of *bhutta* (corn on the cob), pink *cotton candy* (candyfloss), freshly salted *bers* (berries), *kachori* (spicy corn and lentil puffs served with tamarind sauce), *kulfi* (Indian-style ice cream), *chikki* (a nut-based candy) and *mungphali* (peanuts) or *murmura* (puffed rice) packed in slim conical paper pouches. Other common snacks include *samosas* (deep-fried savoury pastries with a spicy potato filling), *pakoras* (batter-dipped vegetable crisps), *cutlets* (flattened fried snacks of meat and potato paste), and *vadas* (deep-fried lentil-flour snacks).

When hunger strikes between meals and there's no *tiffin* around then it can only mean it's *chaat* time. *Chaat* is an omnibus term for a range of superspicy savoury food cooked and hawked on the streets by *chaat wallahs* (spicy food vendors). Each region prides itself on a particular range of *chaat*, although the gamut of *chaat* from all over India can be found on the one *pavement* (footpath). Chief among *chaat* and guaranteed to get your tongue sizzling and your eyes watering are *gol-gappas* (also called *panipuris* and *puchkas*). These are small, lightweight, bubble-shaped savoury items filled with minute portions of spicy sweet-and-sour chutney plus *jal-jeera* (water spiced with cumin and herbs). The little packages are consumed in one bite leading to an explosion of at least ten *chatpata* (zingy) flavours on the palate all at once.

STAPLES

The importance of bread, rice and pulses in India cannot be underestimated – nor can their deliciousness or variety.

Bread

In the north, a dish without bread is like a king without clothes. There are countless variations on the bread theme, some of which are given below:

chapatti   round unleavened bread often eaten with *sabzi* (vegetables) (Hindi)

dosa   a southern Indian rice-lentil pancake (Tamil)

makki ki roti   cornflour *roti* (Hindi)

naan   oven-cooked flatbread (Hindi)

paratha   a *chapatti* fried in *ghee* (clarified butter). A popular version is *aloo paratha* which is stuffed with mashed potato (from Hindi *aloo* 'potato'). (Hindi)

phulka   a dry, puffed *chapatti* (Hindi)

poori   deep-fried puffed round bread, usually eaten with potato *sabzi* (cooked vegetables) (Hindi)

roti   the general term for bread; another word for *chapatti*. Popular versions include *roomali roti* which is a thin bread cooked on an inverted griddle (from Hindi *roomal* 'handkerchief') and *tandoori roti* which is cooked in a *tandoor* oven. (Hindi)

thepla   a wafer-thin *chapatti* eaten with chutney (Gujarati)

Rice

Rice has been cultivated in northern India for at least 7000 years. It was the staple that powered the Indus Valley civilisation that flourished in western India and Pakistan for over a thousand years, starting from about 5000 years ago.

Today rice is consumed in every country on earth and Indians take pride in being the rice-basket of the world. The *basmati* variety of rice, which is grown in the Indo-Gangetic Plain in the north of India, is adored by those who like their rice grains tall and slim, while others prefer their staple short, plump and parboiled. The south–north divide sees rampant racism when it comes to rice. Southerners like it brown, while northerners prefer white.

There's much more to rice, however, than the plain boiled stuff. Apart from *biryani* (fragrant rice casseroles available in vegetarian and nonvegetarian forms) and *pilau* (spicy rice with vegetables), there is *bisi bele baath* (a spicy Bangalore rice dish), *curd rice* (cooked rice mixed with spices, salt and yogurt – in the north it's mixed on your plate and eaten with pickles, while in Bengal you munch it with sugar), *thayiru-sadham* (curd rice with seasoning in Tamil Nadu), *puliyogarai* (tamarind rice, which is great for long journeys as the sourness of the tamarind keeps the rice from rotting), *tomato rice* (cooked rice added into a tomato and spice mixture), *pa-chor* (rice cooked in milk with a pinch of sugar in Kerala) and *ghee rice* (rice cooked with a spicy onion and ghee mixture – the dish is called *nei-chor* in Kerala).

Pulses

Pulses are an important staple across India and are a source of protein for India's many vegetarians. Southern Indians enjoy *sambaar* (a lentil and vegetable curry), whereas northern Indian favourites are *kadi-chawal* (rice with a sauce of yogurt and lentil flour) and *rajma-chawal* (a rice and kidney bean curry).

Here are some terms related to pulses to get you started:

chhole	a favourite North Indian dish with pulses (Hindi)
chana dhal	chickpea (Hindi)
gram	beans, lentils or any other pulses (from Latin via Portuguese)
masur dhal	red lentils (Hindi)
mung dhal	golden or green mung beans (Hindi)
rajma dhal	kidney beans (Hindi)
toor dhal	yellow pigeon peas; also called *arhar* (Hindi)
urad dhal	black mung beans (Hindi)

CONDIMENTS

To make your dish even more flavoursome, and impress the locals at the same time, try asking for some of these tasty additives:

aavakai	a dried mango pickle from Andhra Pradesh (Andhra)
achar	pickles (Hindi)
amchur	powdered dried green mangoes (Hindi)
jeera	cumin seeds, used for seasoning, mostly in the north (Hindi)
kala namak	rock salt (Hindi)
kali mirch	black pepper (Hindi)
mustard seed	used for seasoning, mostly in the South (Indian English)
murabba	a preserved gooseberry, mango or lime relish (Urdu)

VEGETARIAN FARE

Vegetarians in India will always be able to find a sympathetic chef who is used to cooking for people of different religions, each with its attendant prohibitions of this or that ingredient. In India, vegetarians range from *pure vegetarians* (vegans) to *eggetarians* (those who eat eggs). Nonvegetarians can be *fishitarians*, meaning they eat seafood but not other meats. Then there are the *fruitarians* who survive on fruit only. Some Hindus will enjoy cleansing stints of fruitarianism lasting a few days or weeks. Generally speaking, however, it is the eggetarians who dominate the dinner table.

Perusing the menu in an Indian eatery might bring to light some of these vegetarian dishes and ingredients:

akoori	scrambled eggs (originally a Parsi dish) (Gujarati)
aloo dum	a spicy fried new-potato dish (a Kashmiri delicacy)
aloo gobi	a potato and cauliflower dish (Hindi)
arecanut	a nut from the arecanut palm used as a spice
badam	almonds (Hindi)
bhujia	scrambled eggs with onions, coriander leaves and chillies
copra	dried coconut
curry leaves	the leaves of the curry tree used for seasoning throughout India

Food

dahi	yogurt (Hindi)
egg masala	a dish of spicy boiled eggs (Hinglish, from Hindi *masala* 'spice')
egg roast	a spicy dish made with boiled eggs
jaggery	unrefined sugar (Indian English)
kesar	saffron (Hindi)
kishmish	raisins (Urdu)
mulligatawny	a hot pepper soup (from Tamil *milaku* 'pepper' and *tanni* 'water')
namkeen	salty snacks (Hindi)
nariyal paani	coconut water, a fresh drink peddled on most Indian streets (Hindi)
paneer	cottage cheese (Hindi, from Urdu)
ragi	finger millet (Kannada)
rava	semolina (Marathi)
rumble tumble	spicy scrambled eggs
sarson da saag	a dish with mustard leaves, eaten with **makki ki roti** (cornflour bread) (Punjabi)
suji	semolina (Hindi)
thali	a pre-prepared plate with portions of rice, **roti**, **sabzi**, yogurt, salads and sweets (Hindi)
til	sesame seeds (Hindi)

NONVEGETARIAN FARE

For carnivorous types and *fishitarians*, Indian menus usually offer a number of choices:

bombay duck	a small saltwater fish, also called *bombil* (Indian English)
dhansak	spicy, sweet-and-sour dish with meat or prawns (Gujarati)
halal	meat from animals slaughtered in accordance with Muslim law
hilsa	a type of freshwater fish preferred by Bengalis (Bengali)
keema	mincemeat (Hindi)

mughlai	items from the Mughal era like **Shahi-paneer** (royal cottage cheese) (Hindi)
murg	fowl (Hindi)
mutton do piazza	a North Indian mutton dish (from Hindi *do* 'two' and *piazza* 'onions')
mutton korma	mutton cooked with a thick spicy gravy (Hinglish)
pomfret	a type of ocean fish (Indian English)
rogan josh	mutton cooked with intensely hot and fragrant spices (Urdu)
rohu	carp (Bengali)

SWEETS

Indians are enamoured with *mithai* (sweets). These intensely sugary munchies can be an acquired taste, but one which has certainly been acquired by the masses in India. As well as satisfying the sweet tooth, *mithai* are exchanged between friends and relatives on festival days.

Mithai come in many forms and are usually made by a *halwai* (sweet-shop man), who can be spotted stirring milk in a large, flat saucepan, which thickens to make *khoya* – the base for most sweets of northern India. In the south, sweets are predominantly made with rice flour. Popular confections include *barfi* (a fudge-like concoction), *gulab jamun* (deep fried balls of milk dough flavoured with rose-water) and *pazham-pori* (banana fritter). *Laddoos* are ball-shaped flour-based sweetmeats but the word is also slang for 'an obese person', which comes from the expression *gol* (round) *like a laddoo*. This phrase can also be used as a term of endearment, as in *you're so sweet, my laddoo*. Below are a few more verbal sweet treats:

halwa a sticky sweet which can be made with vegetables, cereals, lentils, nuts or fruit (Hindi)

kulfi Indian ice cream made from reduced milk and flavoured with nuts, fruit or berries (Hindi)

kheer a runny rice pudding made with reduced milk and flavoured with cardamom, saffron, pistachios, almonds or dried fruit (Hindi)

payasam the southern Indian name for *kheer* (Sanskrit)

CULINARY ENCOUNTERS

For English colonialists, the encounter with Indian cuisine was a profoundly palate-enriching experience. They took their new-found tastes back to the heart of the Empire, which resulted in these additions to the English culinary lexicon:

curry a heavily spiced sauce or relish made with curry powder and eaten with rice, meat, fish or other food (from Tamil *kari*)

ghee a clarified, semi-fluid butter used a lot in Indian cooking (from Hindi *ghi*, from Sanskrit *gharati* 'sprinkle')

kebab a dish of small pieces of meat and/or vegetables, cooked on skewers (from Urdu/Farsi *kabab* 'roasted meat')

kedgeree a dish of rice, fish and hard-boiled eggs, often served for breakfast. In northern India *kedgeree* refers to a mixture of rice cooked with butter, *dhal*, spices and shredded onions. (From Hindi *khichdi*.)

BREATH FRESHENERS & DIGESTIVES

Excessive heat in the stomach is a cause of bad breath. This might explain why Indians, famous for their curry, traditionally round off a meal by munching on *paan* (a mixture of various ingredients which may or may not include tobacco and betel nut). Not only does its spicy fragrance work like a breath freshener, it also aides digestion. The optional betel nut ingredient in *paan* is also mildly narcotic. Across the nation *paan* is the one vice people cannot resist. Luckily, it's found cheaply on every street corner. In railway stations, red stains on the platforms from the betel nut in *paan* are the blight of station managers.

Other chewy and suckable after-dinner delights include:

chooran a digestive, advertised in some places as *pathar hajam*, *lakkad hajam* 'with this, digest even stones and wood' – still to be medically verified though (Hindi)

elaichi cardamom flakes (Hindi)

mouth freshener breath freshener (Indian English)

mukhwas a digestive made with fennel seeds and various other ingredients (Gujarati)

paan a mix of tobacco, edible limestone, cardamom, arecanut and various other ingredients wrapped in a betel-nut leaf, nowadays offered fresh, chilled or dry as *paans* go designer (Hindi)

paan-masala a mixture containing the mildly narcotic *gutka* (a betel-nut preparation), which is banned in some places in India (Hindi)

saunf fennel (Hindi)

zarda chewing tobacco; can cause giddiness and vomiting in the uninitiated (Urdu)

TUMMY TIME

It's a truism to say that Indians love their food. Stomach-centric sayings abound:

bhukkad	a glutton (Hindi)
glut	a shortened version of the English 'glutton'
khaata-peeta type	a foodie (Hinglish, from Hindi *khaata* 'eating' and *peeta* 'drinking')
mice running in my tummy	'I'm starving', a literal translation of the Hindi saying *pet mein choohe daud rahe hein*
petu	a hearty eater (Hindi, from *pet* 'stomach')

Coconut chutney

Serves three to four people.

½ coconut
small piece ginger
1 green chilly
1 teaspoon mustard seeds
1 small onion
5 or 6 curry leaves
3 or 4 dried red chillies

Method

This is an easy one to get you started. Grind coconut, ginger bits, green chillies (one or two), plus salt to taste, into a coarse or fine paste. While the fine paste makes a *loose chutney*, the coarse grinding is for a *tight chutney*. For seasoning, cook mustard seeds, finely diced onions, curry leaves and dried red chillies in heated oil, then add to paste.

Raita (yogurt-based gravy)

Serves two.

1 cup fresh yogurt
1 onion
1 tomato
1 small cucumber
1 boiled potato (optional)
coriander leaves
salt to taste
red chilli powder to taste

Method

Here is another one before you get cracking on the main menu. Beat yogurt, add sliced onions, tomatoes, cucumber and coriander leaves. Add boiled potato cut into small pieces (optional). Sprinkle with salt and red chilli powder.

Idli (steamed rice flour balls)

2 cups rice
1 cup black lentils, peeled
salt

Method

Soak the rice and black lentils separately for 6 to 7 hours then grind the soaked rice to a coarse paste and the black lentils into a fine paste. Mix the two and leave overnight to ferment. Next morning, add salt to taste, ladle the batter into an *idli*-mould and steam for ten to fifteen minutes. Serve with *sambaar* and coconut chutney.

Sambaar (curry with lentils and vegetables)

Serves two to three people.

1 cup *toor dhal* (pigeon peas)
4 to 5 cups water
sambaar powder (Lightly roast 1 teaspoon turmeric, ½ teaspoon fenugreek, 1 large pinch asafetida, 1 tablespoon coriander seeds, 2 dry red chillies. Grind to a powder after the roasting is done and keep aside.)
1 small ball of tamarind
chopped vegetables (2 small carrots, 2 small potatoes, 1 small yam, 1 small eggplant, 4 to 6 whole shallots)
1 teaspoon mustard seeds
3 or 4 dry red chillies
curry leaves
1 teaspoon oil
salt to taste

Method

Wash and slightly overcook the *toor dhal* in water. Add chopped vegetables and curry leaves. Boil until vegetables are cooked. Add tamarind juice and *sambaar* powder. Remove from heat. To garnish, put mustard seeds and dry red chillies in steaming hot oil until the seeds start to pop, then pour this on the *sambaar*. Serve with rice or *idli*.

FOREIGN INFLUENCES

In urban areas, Indian cuisine competes with Italian-, Chinese, Arabic-, and American-style fast-food outlets. Junk food, especially the burger, is gaining in popularity. To cater for the non-beef-eating Hindu fast-food fanatics, McDonald's offers vegetable burgers as opposed to hamburgers. Pizzas (pronounced 'pi·sas' or 'pi·jas'), lasagne, macaroni, noodles, spaghetti, *chips* (crisps), ice creams, colas and salads are gobbled up by the adventurous Indian palate. And, just as Indian curry tastes different in a Birmingham bistro, the stir-fried noodles in India taste nothing like they would in Shanghai. Food is served with a distinctly Indian flavour – Chinese noodles with *masala* (spices), *paneer pijas* (cottage cheese-topped pizzas), and pasta with Indian herbs are guaranteed to stir your taste buds.

Along with *puffs* and *patties* (both pastries with fillings), bakeries offer made-to-order sandwiches, quiches, brownies, marshmallows and apple pies. Supermarket shelves nowadays are bursting with imported goodies. Despite the premium prices, the perceived quality of products made abroad has ensured good returns for retailers.

Note that the term *bakery items* refers to any snack, while *pastries* are little pieces of cake with colourful icing and *sweetmeats* are simply sweets.

Alcoholic drinks

On average Indians consume far less alcohol than their Western counterparts. A survey conducted in Karnataka state found that 19% of young city folk drank, while only 5% of the population in rural parts consumed liquor. Slum dwellers often fall prey to poisonous *country liquor* (cheap distilled drinks – often illicitly brewed) that can be fatal. Newspapers lament the latest *hooch victims* in stories headlined *Liquor Tragedies*.

At the opposite end of the spectrum are the trendy clubs and bars serving drinks as fashion statements. It is now easy to find a place where you can order cocktails in tall frosted glasses with cute paper umbrellas perched on the rim. In *metro* bars, *bar girls* (women paid to dance in bars, often as a prelude to offering sexual services) are a new phenomenon,

---

SPIRITED HINDI SAYINGS

apni aankhon se pilao	intoxicate me with your eyes
mai ka pyaala	literally 'liquor bowls', but usually refers to a pair of female eyes
na piyo, na pilao	neither drink, nor offer drinks
pee rakhi hai?	'Are you drunk?', often said to someone who is proposing something ridiculous

which has now been banned by the Maharashtrian government. Models and starlets mix cocktails and *mocktails* (sans alcohol) for celebrities and fashionistas.

As the image of drinking becomes less associated with being down and out and more closely aligned to having a good time, people are no longer ashamed to report they are *hanged-over* and the brand-name *daru* (liquor) market is poised for *big-time* growth. In hotels and restaurants watch out for the *Bar-Attached* sign without which liquor cannot be served.

Whiskey, vodka, gin, rum and the rest of the short liquor gang can be found in all the posh bars. Brandy, considered a medicinal draught, is administered to children and the elderly to help combat colds. So far the taste for Champagne and other white wines has proved unpopular among the middle class, which also considers them overpriced. Wine is made only in the grape-growing districts of Maharashtra. The cheap *port wine* sold in Goa is actually alcohol diluted with wine flavouring.

A drunkard is a *piyakkad* (from Hindi *piya* 'drink') or *sharaabi* (from Hindi *sharaab* 'liquor') and is described as *walking on four legs* (crawling), being in *nasha* (an intoxicated daze) or *nashe mein tun* (lost in intoxication). *Drunken driving* refers to accidents in the wake of inebriation. In Kerala, drunks are contradictorily called *fit*.

arrack   a South Indian liquor made from distilled coconut-palm sap and various other ingredients. A *country liquor* to be treated with caution. (Indian English, from Arabic.)

botal   a bottle of liquor (a Hindi borrowing from standard English)

chhota peg   a small portion of liquor (Hinglish, from Hindi *chhota* 'small' and English *peg*) *country liquor*   cheap distilled spirits made from a range of vegetable matter including molasses – the poor man's drink (Indian English)

dry day   national holidays when licensed liquor shops down shutters (Indian English)

feni   Goan alcoholic drink made from cashew-nut juice (Konkani)

hooch   illegally brewed alcohol (Indian English)

Patiala peg   an extra large measure of an alcoholic drink (Indian English; Patiala is a place in Punjab)

port wine   a red wine–flavoured liquor from Goa (Indian English)

sharab   liquor (Urdu)

toddy   called *kallu* down south, it's a liquor prepared from sap tapped from the coconut palm (Indian English, from Hindi *tari* 'palmyra palm juice')

REGIONAL BREWS

Goa is the famous west coast party destination with a unique *chillax* (chilled and relaxed) vibe. *Feni*, the traditional Goan alcohol, flows as freely as the clouds.

In Kerala, it's fresh *toddy* – white-coloured, sweet-and-sour coconut-palm liquor – that bonds the drinkers. The region is also famous for its home-made wines that are made from almost everything in the garden, including leftover rose petals, rice, and gooseberries, along with cashew nuts, cloves and aromatic cinnamon sticks, added for extra flavour.

THIRST QUENCHER

Refrigerated potable water is hawked on Delhi streets with a sign saying *Machine ka Thanda Paani* (cold water from the machine).

In Tamil Nadu quench your thirst with either a cup of *rasam* – a fiery, sour and spicy nonalcoholic drink – or home-made *hooch* in little plastic pouches.

Before Independence, every royal family in Rajasthan produced its own brand of liquor. The 'blue booze' was banned in 1952 when the *Rajasthan Excise Act* came into force. The ban was lifted in 1998 and production permitted under the *desi* (Indian) liquor category. The royal brews listed below sell for between Rs 300 and Rs 3000 per 750mL bottle. The recipes are, of course, closely guarded secrets.

Shyapur Narangi   a spicy ginger and pineapple liquor

Sodawas Mawalin   a liquor made from dates, dried fruits and two dozen secret spices

Mahansar Gulab   a liquor made from fennel, orange, rose, mint and ginger and sold under the brand names Royal Mahansar, Maharani Mahansar and Maharaja Mahansar

Kanota Chandrahas   made from nearly 165 spices, and dried fruits including saffron and gooseberries, *Kanota Chandrahas* is also called the 'liquor of life' as it is rumoured to have revived a king on his deathbed

Nonalcoholic drinks

H_2O is a no go – drinking *pipe* (tap) water could lay you out with jaundice, cholera, diarrhoea and amoebiasis. Even quaffing down unboiled or unfiltered water, or adding impure *barf* (ice) to your drink and sampling water-based snacks, such as *gol-gappas* (deep-fried dough puffs dipped in a spicy water) and *chuski* (crushed coloured ice on a stick) can be bad for health. Instead try *jeera* water (water boiled with cumin seeds), *lassi* (sweet yogurt), *chhachh* (salted buttermilk), bottled mineral water, or water that has been boiled and then cooled in a mud pot, all of which help to wash down meals. Other beverages to choose from include:

Bournvita	a chocolate milk drink (a brand name)
badam milk	cold milk flavoured with saffron and crushed almonds (Hinglish)
cool drink	any soft drink (Indian English)
Horlicks	a hot or cold milk drink made with malt powder (a brand name)
jal-jeera	a refreshing drink flavoured with mint and cumin (Hindi)
kanji-water	a thin, grainless gruel or rice-water, considered a light, nutritious drink for the sick (Keralite Indian English, from Malayalam *kanji* 'water')
kanchi soda	a soft drink sold in a bottle with a marble in its neck which is pushed down in order to open it – often mixed with lime juice or spices, also called *goli soda* (Hinglish, from Hindi *kancha* 'marble')
masala soda	a spiced soda drink (Hinglish, from Hindi *masala* 'spice')

nimbu paani	lemonade (Hindi)
panna	a drink made from green mangoes (Hindi)
Roohafzah	a cooling fuchsia-coloured drink in the north flavoured with rose essence (a brand name)
sherbet	a syrupy drink made from rose essence or almonds (Indian English, from Arabic)

Nonalcoholic drinks

117

TEA

In 1815, when Scotsman Robert Bruce 'discovered' tea growing in Assam, nobody believed him. Even the most cunning horticulturalist was convinced that tea plants could only grow in China. It took his brother Charles almost 20 years to prove to the British Establishment what the locals had known for generations. Today India is the largest tea growing nation in the world. More than 1 million acres of *Camellia sinensis,* more commonly known as tea, are under cultivation.

Chai (tea) is everywhere and it is cheap. It is always drunk at important social, political or academic gatherings. Before it's served, *chai* is poured from one canister to another in rapid succession to create a tasty froth. *Chai-dhabas* (teahouses) are popular meeting places and often open all night. Service is from *tea-boys* who scurry around with trays of steaming tea in glasses (pronounced 'gi·las'). The boys and the tea-stall owners are called *chai-wallahs.*

Aboard trains, tea is served in little mud pots called *kulhads.* Passengers often pour tea from the cups into the accompanying saucers leaving it to cool before sipping straight from the saucer. Up north, tea is flavoured with cardamom, ginger and other spices. It is usually served milky and very sweet.

adrak-waali	tea boiled with ginger shavings to help heal a cold (Hindi)
cutting chai	half a cup of tea (Hinglish, from Hindi *chai* 'tea' and)
chai-paani	a slang expression meaning 'a bribe' (Hindi, literally 'tea-water')
chuski	an onomatopoeic Hindi word meaning 'a sip' – mostly used for a sip of hot tea

elaichi-waali	tea with cardamom (Hindi)
ice-waali	cold tea with ice cubes (Hinglish, from Hindi *waali* 'with')
kadak chai	strong, almost bitter tea (Hindi)
kaali chai	black tea (Hindi)
kaali-mirch chai	black pepper tea, thought to cure colds or sore throats (Hindi)
lemon tea	black tea with lemon juice or rind (Indian English)
malai mar ke	tea with cream, mostly reserved for visitors (Hindi, literally 'hit with cream'; Mumbai slang)
masala chai	highly-spiced tea (Hindi)
panikam-chai	strong tea (from Hindi 'tea with less water'; Mumbai slang)

COFFEE

In cities, the traditional *coffee-house* culture, which saw intellectuals gather in murky state-sponsored environs, can be added to India's store of bygone relics. It has been replaced by city cafés serving the growing middle classes with European style decaf, *caffè latte*, double espresso, cappuccino, mocha and Irish coffee. For the majority of locals, coffee is simply served either *strong* or *light*.

Coffee (pronounced variously 'ko·fi', 'kaa·pi' and 'kaa·fi') is the drink of preference in the south, whereas tea rules in the north. Across the country, most venues and hosts will, however, offer both. Whichever you choose, it is polite to leave the last sip at the bottom of the cup as a *baaki* (remnant).

Tamil Nadu is known as India's coffee capital. Here, coffee is served in tumblers inside steel bowls and made using the traditional technique of *decoction* (brewing) that uses freshly ground whole beans for a supposedly fuller flavour. In the north *cold coffee* (pronounced 'kol ko·fi') is the coffee of choice. It sports a creamy froth at the rim, which lingers lovingly on the moustache.

The following are some common types of coffee in India:

black coffee	coffee without milk (Indian English)
cold coffee	iced coffee (Indian English)
decoction	made by brewing freshly ground coffee beans (Indian English)
instant	coffee powder that dissolves instantly in boiled milk (Indian English)
Madras filter coffee	a strong, sweet, milky coffee made from roasted dark coffee beans with the addition of chicory (Indian English)

SAYING IT WITH FLOWERS

Given the common practice in India of casually adorning hair with hibiscus, rose or jasmine, you'd be forgiven for thinking many heads resemble mobile mini-flowerpots. The following are some useful flower-related terms:

gajra	floral comb for hair, made of fresh flowers, jasmine/marigold; northern usage (Hindi)
mogra	*Jasminum sambac*, jasmine hair comb (Hindi)
morning glory	common creeper sometimes worn in the hair (Indian English)
queen of the night	*Cestrum nocturnum*, flat white flowers that bloom in the night, sometimes worn in the hair (Indian English, also known by the Hindi *raat ki raani* 'queen of the night')
veni	floral comb; southern usage (Sanskrit)

Like every ancient civilisation, India prides itself on a long and honourable tradition of sport. References in early Vedic texts to *dehvada* (the way of the body) indicate physical training was perceived as one of the paths to *nirvana*. Depictions in the *Ramayana* and *Mahabharata* epics (see boxed text p70) reveal that Indian kings held athletic tournaments comparable with the Olympic Games of ancient Greece. Today's athletes are more likely to strive for a gold medal than a more favourable incarnation, but the philosophic tradition of *dehvada* still underpins the nation's most popular export, yoga.

Cricket

Any discussion about sport in India has to begin with cricket. Visitors who exhibit interest in the game will be well received. To say the game is a national obsession is an understatement; when it comes to cricket in India, the distinction between sport and religion is blurred. As soon as they're old enough to bowl, kids from all backgrounds start to play in parks, back lots, alleyways, and the town *maidan* (cricket oval on public grounds). Lack of equipment is no excuse and you'll often spot them using sticks for improvised bats and wickets.

A HAAROFYING LOSS

The generic term for sport in northern India is *khel-khood*, derived from the Hindi *khelna* (to play) and *khoodna* (to jump). In general, southern Indians prefer using the English word 'sport' (always in the singular, as in British English, rather than the American English 'sports'). Throughout the country, you'll often hear of a team *jeetofying* or *haarofying* (Hinglish from the Hindi *jeetna* 'to win' and *haarna* 'to lose').

Cricket

121

FAMOUS CRICKETERS

Once players reach a certain level of cricketing glory in India, they are revered as demigods who can do no wrong. The public follows every aspect of their lives, but they are relatively free of the censure and humiliation that most Bollywood celebrities have to endure at some point – lucky them. Here's a list of those who have attained elite status. Dropping these names into any conversation is a sure way to make new friends.

Anil Kumble
A famous leg-spin bowler (curving the ball from right to left) and one of the highest wicket-takers of all time in India. Captain of the national test cricket team since 2007, he once took an amazing 10 wickets in an innings against Pakistan in 1999.

Diana Eduljee
The first national women's team captain in the 1980s and 1990s, an *all-rounder* (proficient at both batting and bowling).

Kapil Dev
Dubbed the *Haryana Hurricane*, he was an all-rounder and was the highest wicket-taker in the world when he retired from the game. He was team captain when India won the Cricket World Cup in 1983.

Mohammed Azharuddin
Captain of the Indian cricket team during the 1990s, Azharuddin is one of the best batsmen in national history.

Sachin Tendulkar
Superstar batsman who earned the moniker *Master Blaster*, he has scored over 10,000 runs in both forms of the game, ie five-day test matches and one-day internationals.

Sourav Ganguly
Captain of the Indian cricket team from 2000 until 2005, the left-handed Bengali batsman was known for dominating bowlers.

Rahul Dravid
A technically outstanding, defensive player, known less for fireworks than for reliability. He also served as the captain of the Indian squad up until 2007.

Sunil Gavaskar
The diminutive batsman, whose heyday was in the 1970s and 1980s, was the first in the world to reach 10,000 test runs.

The 'Spin Quartet'
Erapalli Prasanna, Bishan Singh Bedi, S Venkataraghavan, Bhagwat Chandrasekhar – a band of bowlers, who, during their prime (from the late 1960s through the entire 1970s), were regarded as the best bowling line-up worldwide.

Not surprisingly, every member of the national cricket team has celebrity status. If the first eleven formed a boy band, the resulting pandemonium would be unprecedented. Major tournaments require that the nation's business activities and social pursuits grind to a halt. It is not unusual for employees to secure leave for the World Cup months in advance – often needlessly, as their bosses may be 'sick' anyway when India's playing. During international matches the entire country gets hysterical, regardless of whether India *jeetofies* or *haarofies*. Probably the most acceptable excuse for turning up late for an appointment is that you couldn't tear yourself away from a particularly close match.

Occasionally, cricket has been a dividing force in Indian society. When India plays Pakistan, some Indian Muslims are reported to support the Pakistani side – a state of affairs that infuriates many Hindus. However, most would argue that cricket serves to unite the country both physically (in the stands) and metaphorically. Not only does it provide a common subject to talk about, it helps to heal political divisions as well. Pundits point to the India–Pakistan series of 2005 as a great diplomatic moment between the two nations. Both nations treated opposing players and fans with extreme courtesy and many friendships were forged during this tournament.

The uninitiated often complain that cricket matches are about as thrilling as watching paint dry. Expressing such a view while in India is not recommended. Instead, get to understand the basic rules of the game and try joining in the mania.

Cricket is played by two teams using a bat (confusingly referred to by the Hindi term **balla**) and a very hard ball. One team takes the field and bowls while the other team bats. The pivotal players are the bowler and the batsman. The object of the game is to score more runs than the other side. After they hit the ball, the batsmen can run back and forth along the bowling pitch as long as the ball is in play and, each time this happens, a run is scored. If the batsman hits the ball all the way to the edge of the field, he scores four runs automatically. This is called a **chauka** (from the Hindi *chaar* 'four'). If the batsman hits the ball out of the field without the ball touching the ground, that's a sixer (**chhakka** in colloquial Hindi), or knocked for six.

It is the job of the bowling team to prevent the batting team from scoring runs by catching or bowling them **out**. The bowler delivers the ball in the batsman's direction using a windmill-like throwing motion, as the bowling arm must be kept straight during delivery. To bowl a player out, the bowler must throw the ball so that it bounces and then hits the **wicket**, a structure behind the batsman of the opposing team that consists of three **stumps** (stakes driven into the ground) and two **bails** (cylinders) balanced on the stumps.

Of course, not all is fun and games for the batsmen. There are several ways to end a play. If a batsman's ball is caught before it hits the ground, the batsman is *caught out*. If a fielder knocks the bails off the stumps while the batsman is running, the batsman is *run out*. If this happens before running commences, the batsman is *stumped*. If the bowler knocks the bails off with a well-bowled ball, the batsman has been *bowled*. Finally, if the ball hits the batsman's leg and the umpire deems that it would have hit the wicket had the leg not been in the way, the batsman is out by *lbw* (leg before wicket).

Bowlers use a variety of methods to get the ball past the batsman. *Spin bowlers* rely on strange, twisty ball bounces, while *pace bowlers* send the ball as fast as possible, blazing a path to the wicket. The Hindi word *doosra* (meaning 'second' or 'other') has been adopted into English cricket parlance and refers to a particularly confusing ball that bounces the opposite way from what is expected.

Excited yet? Any time is a good time to watch cricket in India. While the main international season runs from August to April, various tournaments occur year-round. Some major national tournaments include the *Ranji Trophy*, the *Duleep Trophy* and the *Deodhar Trophy*.

For an insight into just how profoundly cricket is imbued in local culture, check out the award-winning film

THE VOICE OF A NATION

Cricket's widespread popularity will forever be associated with *AFS Talyarkhan*, who provided *the* voice of cricket to the nation. The radio commentator's refined manner belied a consuming passion for the game. 'Bobby', as he was affectionately known, brought a phenomenal amount of knowledge, anecdotes and stamina to the airwaves. He never shared the microphone and his broadcasts would last into the wee hours. Even though his final broadcast was in 1949, journalists and other commentators constantly sought his expert opinion until his passing in 1990.

Lagaan (Tax), the story of an Indian village that tries to win economic independence from oppressive colonialists via a cricket match.

Cricket is big business in India. The new Indian Premier League pays millions of US dollars in salaries – far more than any other sport in the nation. The temptation to gamble on the results is too great in many instances, and several players and captains have been accused of match-fixing over the last few decades.

Yoga

Undoubtedly one of India's great contributions to global culture, yoga philosophy and practice continue to radiate from the mother country like harmonious ripples across a pond. The word *yoga* is a Sanskrit term meaning 'union', related to the now rarely used sense of the English word 'yoke' to mean a link or bond. Historically, yoga is the attempt to reunite the *Atman* (individual spirit) with *Brahman* (the great divine force of the universe) using various physical and mental techniques. If you are a *yogi* or *yogini* (male or female practitioner of yoga respectively), much of the Sanskrit-derived vocabulary will be familiar.

The forms of yoga most prevalent in the West stem from *hatha yoga*. The goal of this discipline is to achieve wellbeing by coordinating body, mind and spirit through breathing techniques and various *asanas* (postures). Beginners usually take to *iyengar yoga*, which places a great deal of emphasis on proper form and technique with slow transitions between asanas. For the more active, *ashtanga yoga* relies on quick movements and strenuous exercises to increase strength and flexibility. *Bikram yoga* is a relatively new phenomenon and is a rigorous school of yoga conducted in special heated rooms. This is perplexing to many Indians, who tend to practise yoga in the cooler mornings. *Bhakti yoga* emphasises the spiritual element and is essentially a form of devotional worship. *Tantric yoga's* sexual connotations have given it a dubious reputation in the West, but it properly refers to techniques that allow the body to harness hidden energies, sexual ones included.

An *ashram* is any place of spiritual retreat and, especially, a place where yoga is studied. If you visit an ashram, you are likely to encounter yoga students following the precepts of one or two *swamis* (masters) or *gurus* (teachers). When deep in meditation, the students may be chanting *mantras*, which are holy utterances designed to centre the mind for meditation. The most famous mantra, which also happens to serve as the symbol for Hinduism, is *Aum* (also called *Om*) – a sound that is supposed to unite the three stages of the universe: creation, preservation and destruction.

Hockey

When British army regiments introduced the modern game of hockey to India, they could not have guessed that within a few decades the Indians would be the world force in the sport. From 1928, the Indian men's team won six straight Olympic gold titles. For much of the 20th century the Indian and Pakistani teams dominated the field until rule changes in the 1970s and 1980s tipped the balance in favour of bigger athletes and wealthier teams. Formerly a game played barefoot on grass, professional field hockey is now played on synthetic surfaces with harder sticks and at a faster pace. Many Indians long for the good old days, when skill and agility, rather than speed and strength, determined the winners, and when teams didn't have to scrimp and save to afford a synthetic playing surface.

GO FOR IT, INDIA

Blockbuster *Chak De! India* (Go for it, India; 2007) had superstar Shahrukh Khan playing an ex-hockey captain who coaches the Indian women's national hockey team to victory in Australia.

India's most famous hockey player is **Dhyan Chand** – dubbed the **Indian Wizard** – who was a star of the 1920s and 1930s. His ball control was so phenomenal that opposing teams accused him of concealing magnets or using glue. An admiring Adolf Hitler reportedly offered him a position in the German army, which Chand declined. Also well known is **Ajitpal Singh**, who captained the Indian team in the 1970s and was widely regarded as the best player of his day. He was raised in the village of Sansarpur, which has turned out a disproportionately high number of world-class hockey players. Another famous Indian hockey player of the 1970s is **Aslam Sher Khan**, who was a star defender in many of India's Olympic medal teams and later successfully entered politics.

Hockey's heyday in India is over, but several domestic tournaments provide ample opportunities to enjoy the sport, including the **Maharaja Ranjeet Singh Hockey Tournament** and the **Beighton Cup**. Matches played by teams in the **Premier Hockey League** are always a blast.

Football

Football (soccer) may run a distant third to cricket and hockey in the pantheon of Indian team sports, but don't try telling that to its devotees. The enmity between opposing teams in Kolkata rivals the bad blood that exists between teams in the European leagues. The most intense domestic rivalries are between the three Kolkata teams of the **National Football League**, namely **Mohun Bagan**, **East Bengal** and **Mohammedan Sporting**. A match between any two of these clubs is guaranteed to be a spectacle with more than 100,000 fans in attendance. Indian football tournaments include the *Durand Cup*, *Santosh Trophy*, and *Federation Cup*. The domestic league received a massive boost in December 2007 when the Portuguese League for Professional Football (LPFP) signed an agreement with the *All Indian Football Federation* (AIFF) to provide financial support for a more professional structure.

Grassroots football is huge in eastern India, especially in the state of West Bengal. Goa and Kerala also boast impressive local teams. As it's a relatively cheap sport to play (only one ball is required), football is a perfect pastime for street-kids playing barefoot – the Indian national team played without boots until the 1960s.

Famous football personalities include *Pradip Kumar Banerjee*, who coached the national team in the 1960s after a stellar international career (which won him the FIFA Indian Footballer of the 20th Century award); *Invalappil Mani Vijayan*, a star striker for several Kolkatan and Goan teams in the 1990s; and *Bhaichung Bhutia*, a Sikkimese striker who occasionally played in England in the 1990s.

Kabaddi

If, while in India, you switch on the TV and see what appears to be a large group of people imitating chimpanzees, loping about and making threatening gestures at each other, don't be alarmed. Chances are it's not a lame re-enactment of *Planet of the Apes* – you're witnessing a *kabaddi* match.

Hugely popular in rural parts, kabaddi is a home-grown game that rivals any international sport for excitement and suspense. It is played on a large field or pitch – often cricket *maidans* are used. Two teams occupy opposite halves of the pitch. They then take it in turns to send a player, called a *raider*, into the other team's half. If the raider *tags* (touches) an opposing team member and returns to his or her half within an allotted time, the raider's team scores a point. If a player from the defending team manages to *hold* the raider, preventing him or her from returning back to the attacking half, then the defending team scores a point. Any contact between the raider and the defending team is called a *contest*.

The catch is how the allotted time is determined – it's not by a clock! Rather, players must accomplish their missions all in one breath. That is, they are not allowed to breathe during the entire time they are in the opposing half. In order to prove that they are not breathing, raiders are required to chant *kabaddi kabaddi kabaddi* at a furious pace while performing their missions.

Kabaddi is most popular in Punjab, which boasts a couple of regional leagues and corporate sponsors. Elsewhere it is mainly an informal event, used to promote friendly competition between neighbouring villages. In southern India, kabaddi is known as *hu tu tu* (and the breathless chant is altered accordingly).

Racquet sports

When it comes to hitting balls with racquets, Indians have always performed well on the world stage. The most watched racquet sport in India is tennis. Although Indian players haven't had much recent success on the Grand Slam circuit, the national tennis stars are adored. The most famous Indian tennis player was probably *Vijay Amritraj*, who had a reputation for being a giant killer (his scalps included Björn Borg, Rod Laver and John McEnroe). Along with his brother *Anand*, he achieved success in the doubles category in the late 1970s. Amritraj's success spurred him to Hollywood, where he appeared in the James Bond film *Octopussy* and *Star Trek IV: The Voyage Home*.

Ramesh Krishnan (son of tennis great, *Ramanathan Krishnan*) was India's best player during the late 1980s and early 1990s. Despite his best efforts, he failed to win a Grand Slam tournament and faded from international competition by 1995. His mantle has passed to *Leander Paes* from Goa, and *Mahesh Bhupathi* from Bangalore. Both players have put in strong doubles performances at the French Open and Wimbledon.

Female tennis stars have been few and far between. *Nirupama Mankad* was India's first female star, attaining fame in the Asian competition, and a modicum of success on the international stage. Bizarrely, the heir to her title of best Indian female, *Nirupama Vaidyanathan*, bears the same first name. More recently hopes are pinned on *Sania Mirza.*

Badminton is second to tennis in Indian hearts. The 1980s were India's golden era with *Prakash Padukone* destroying the competition at the All England Open and Swedish Open in the first year of the decade. The current rising stars are *Saina Nehwal* and *Anup Sridhar*, both of whom seem destined for great things.

CHILD'S PLAY

When there aren't enough kids around to make up a cricket team, *gilli-danda* is the popular alternative. Players compete by using a long, straight stick (the *danda* 'stick') to flick a wooden cylinder (the *gilli* 'block') into the air. They then use the *danda* to hit the *gilli* as far as possible. Whoever hits the *gilli* farthest is the winner.

Another widespread game is *kho-kho*, which is vaguely similar to tag. A *chaser*, assisted by team-mates, attempts to touch as many defenders as possible inside a small space. It sounds simple but it's complicated enough to have several leagues as well as a national competition (among adults).

An insensitively named game called *langari* (literally 'lame person') is a cousin of *kho-kho*. In *langari*, the attacking player must chase defenders while hopping on one leg. Continuing the hopping theme, *tipri* is an indigenous form of hopscotch that's played with small stones to indicate where to jump.

In most of the country badminton is played with a shuttlecock (called a *birdie*), but in the south it's often played using a *gend* (small ball). When played with a *gend* the game is known as *ball badminton*.

Table tennis, affectionately known as *TT*, is another favourite. Interest is most keen when the national team plays neighbouring rival China.

Athletics

India's tendency of dwelling on the accomplishments of legends from the distant past has not helped prepare new generations for athletics success. Despite an acknowledgement of this by a number of cultural critics, it doesn't pay to be outspoken on the issue. An Indian candidate for Miss Universe was dropped from the competition after voicing her frustration with the Athletics Federation of India (AFI). When asked about the one thing she would fight for if crowned, she replied that she would strive for better sports facilities in her home country. She might have fared better by saying 'world peace'.

Despite the obstacles, India manages to acquit itself reasonably well in international competition. India's biggest star is *Anju Bobby George*. The female long jumper won bronze at the 2003 IAAF World Championships in Athletics in Paris before achieving silver at the IAAF World Athletics Final in 2005.

Officials are hoping to use India's respectable showing in the 2006 Commonwealth Games, which included a haul of 16 gold medals, to train a new generation of athletes. There are great expectations for the new breed to come into their own in time for the 2010 Commonwealth Games in New Delhi.

Other sports

Polo originated on the steppes of Central Asia, but it was India that introduced the 'sport of kings' to the West. During the time of the British Raj, polo was adopted by army generals after observing Indian nobility playing their version of 'field hockey with horses' throughout the land. Today, India is one of only a handful of nations that boasts a professional polo league. The Hindi term *chukker* (roughly meaning 'a round') is the official British English name for a period of play in polo. *Elephant polo*, which was invented in India, is now rarely played, although Sri Lanka and Nepal both have professional leagues.

The only martial art indigenous to India is *kalaripayattu*, which is practised in the southern state of Kerala. Lauded by its proponents as one of the earliest forms of martial art, *kalaripayattu* is a Malayalam term that means 'training in the gymnasium.' These days, *kalaripayattu* is more likely to be performed as a demonstration sport than as a self-defence technique. It involves graceful, dancelike movements and fluid pacing.

Kushti is an Indian form of wrestling that resembles the Greco-Roman version practised during the ancient Olympic Games. The object is to contort the opponent's body until they fall down and can be pinned flat on the ground. A practitioner of *kushti* is known as a *pehelwan*.

Jallikattu is a variant on bullfighting 'played' in Tamil Nadu and Andhra Pradesh. In this particularly deadly form of the sport, humans are more likely to suffer fatalities than the bull. Prizes, usually bundles of cash, are tied to the horns of a bull, which is then set loose in a village. Several unarmed and unarmoured men chase the bull and attempt to control it by grasping its horns and wrestling the animal into submission. Whoever subdues the bull may untie the prize and claim victory. Participating cattle are decorated with garlands, horns are painted and mango leaves hung from their necks before the *jallikattu* begins. Associated village-carnival events, such as bullock cart races and cockfights, are also held during the time of *jallikattu*.

For some reason, India has always done well at billiards, producing such legendary champions as **Wilson Jones** who became the first Indian to win the International Billiards and Snooker Federation (IBSF) World Billiards Championships in 1958. **Geet Sethi** won the same championship three times and came second three times, and **Michael Ferreira**, nicknamed the **Bombay Tiger**, won the championship three times and came second twice and relentlessly campaigned for billiards to be treated as cricket's equal – maybe one day.

The Persian and Arabian Empires credited India with inventing chess. By the 6th century AD the precursor to the modern game, *chaturanga*, was being played in India. India has only managed one chess world-beater and superstar: **Vishwanath Anand**, the grandmaster, won the World Chess Championship in 2007 and was number one in the world in the World Chess Federation (FIDE) rankings for most of that year.

Recent years have seen Indian athletes take on the world's best at shooting and weightlifting. Current sharpshooters include **Samaresh Jung**, who was presented with the David Dixon Award for the most outstanding athlete of the 2006 Commonwealth Games, **Vivek Singh**, **Gagan Narang**, **Rajyavardhan Singh Rathore** and **Tejaswini Sawant**. The national women's weightlifting team comprises **Shailaja Pujari**, **Pratima Kumari**, **Sanamacha Chanu**, and **Kunjarani Devi Nameirakpam**. Along with their sole male counterpart **Satheesha Rai**, every member of the squad has won gold at the Commonwealth Games within the past decade.

India's entertainment industry is growing by the minute. Cable TV, shopping malls, movie halls and pubs are all being modernised to accommodate an increasingly globalised palate. Nightlife, however, continues to be unpredictable in the country with some cities downing shutters by 6pm or 7pm, with others staying opening till all hours. Entertainment can vary wildly – from a bunch of boys playing cricket in a narrow bylane to a group of techies (software engineers) applauding professional players on a giant plasma TV screen in a pub.

Movies

In India, entertainment equals *Bollywood*, the Mumbai-centred Hindi-language film sector. This thriving industry worth big bucks used to be mocked for its over-the-top, all-singing, all-dancing dramatic portrayals. My, how the tables have turned. Flagrant rip-offs by Bollywood of Hollywood classics such as *The Godfather* and *Reservoir Dogs* are embarrassing relics of the past. Now Hollywood seeks guidance and inspiration from its Indian peers. The runaway Hindi hit *Munnabhai MBBS* is all set for a Hollywood remake.

Labyrinthine plots, heroic acts by lead actors in the face of danger and, of course, song and dance are the key ingredients that keep audiences enthralled. The magic of Bollywood cuts across barriers of age, caste and economic status.

To keep pace with rapid developments in Indian English and grab the attention of non-Indian markets, movies are now often made either completely in English or in Hinglish, using mixed dialogues in Hindi and English. The Hinglish movies are adored by domestic audiences as it is the natural dual mode of speaking in many parts of India.

Movies

For films in Hindi or other Indian languages (see box p137), catchy English titles such as *Page 3*, *Joggers' Park*, and *Jhankar Beats* abound. This is despite protests from 'purists' who would prefer English to be dropped from Indian films altogether.

Movie critics have moved on from lamenting the use of any English, to accepting the use of Hinglish without Hindi subtitles. The incursion of Hinglish began with the *villain* mouthing exclamations such as *dammit*, *bastard* and *bloody fool* and evolved to the current situation where whole exchanges take place in English. It was the multiplex market that finally destroyed the Hindi-exclusivity myth completely, following the box-office success of turn-of-the-millennium films like *Hazaron Khwaishein Aisi*, which has Hindi, English and Punjabi combining to form a heady linguistic cocktail sans apology.

Filmmakers such as Mira Nair, Gurinder Chadha, and Nagesh Kukunoor who wrote entire scripts in English are the creators and perpetrators of a new style: the *crossover film*. A distinctive feature of this genre is the injection of realism into the erstwhile *masala potboiler* formula – all the usual elements that go into making a hit in India, like a sexy dance number, some memorable dialogue, and multiple stars.

Today, it's not just the villains but also the heroes who freely mouth Indian English, and no seduction routine is now complete without the English words *hello baby* and *come on*. Incidentally, the hero in Indian movies is usually a *chikna* (smooth-shaven hunk) as mustachioed men mostly fail as Indian sex symbols (at least in the North). The leading man's success also depends on his *chocolate boy* (seductively appealing) looks.

Though come-on lines might be in Indian English, taboos regarding public displays of affection prevent the unbridled expression of passion on the Indian silver screen. Lip-to-lip kissing was, until recently, banned by the Central Board of Film Certification (CBFC) as 'alien to Indian culture'. *Lip-lock* – where actors just rest their lips against each other's in a staged attempt at a kiss – has been an alternative tolerated by the morality police. The situation is still, however, volatile. A *lip-lock* exchange between an Indian actor and a Pakistani actress once sparked a cross-border diplomatic controversy between the rival powers, and a kiss between Bollywood heart-throb Hrithik Roshan and Aishwarya Rai in *Dhoom 2* (2006) unleashed a media storm. It seems inevitable that, in the not too distant future, a real scorcher of a smooch will set matinée marquees ablaze, maybe literally.

BOLLYWOOD, KOLLYWOOD, TOLLYWOOD…

If you're having trouble seeing the forest for all the '-wood', here's a description of all the major Indian film industries to help you out:

Assamese cinema films have been made in the Assamese language since 1935

Bengali cinema there are two branches of the Bengali-language film industry: one based in Tollygunge, Kolkata, called *Tollywood*, the other, called *Dhallywood*, based in Dhaka, Bangladesh

Bollywood the world-renowned Hindi-language film industry; a word coined from a combination of Bombay and Hollywood

Cinema of Karnataka the Karnataka film industry primarily releases films in the Kannada language

Kollywood the Tamil-language film industry; the word Kollywood derives from a combination of Kodambakkam, Chennai (formerly Madras), where most Kollywood films are produced, and Hollywood

Lollywood the Pakistani film industry, which mainly produces films in Urdu. The term Lollywood comes from a combination of Hollywood and Lahore, the city where the industry is based.

Malayalam cinema the Malayalam-language film industry based in Kerala

Marathi cinema the Marathi-language film industry based in Mumbai

Punjwood the Punjabi-language film industry, also called *Pollywood*

Tollywood the Telugu-language film industry, or the Bengali film industry based in Kolkata

Dramatic dialogues can sometimes be a bit over the top. People are dismissed as *filmi* when they get too melodramatic or filmlike. The theatrical type is warned against *dialogue-baazi* (from Hindi *baazi* 'indulgence'), as if after delivering the line they are waiting for *taaliyan* (applause). In the cinema you'll often hear members of the audience inquiring *who's the heroine?* (lead actress) or *hero* (lead actor) – meaning they think that the intended lead actors are not conventionally handsome or young enough and should be classified as character actors and not lead actors. A particularly tragic lament would be that *the film has no heroine* – meaning it bucks the trend of conventional Indian films, which usually have a hero, a heroine, a villain and a car chase. Without a heroine there is, much to the chagrin of audiences, less scope for song and dance.

Enjoyment rests mainly on effective *dialogue-baazi* (dialogue delivery) as audiences demand a *mast* (fun) script.

Here's some more cinematic vocabulary:

art films   mostly award-winning films, which are generally panned by the masses but watched by the upper classes

character artiste   an actor in a substantial, but not lead, role

cinemascope   a large screen in a movie hall

dinchak   onomatopoeia for a beating sound, a slang word for loud disco music (Hindi)

dhak-dhak   bosom-heaving   by   a   *heroine*   (Hindi onomatopoeia for the sound of a heart beating)

dhoom machana   having fun (Hindi)

dishum   onomatopoeia for the hero's punch landing on the *villain's* stomach

double role   a lead actor playing two roles simultaneously in a common ploy to popularise the film; the late actor Sanjeev Kumar played no less than nine roles simultaneously in *Naya Din, Nayi Raat* (New Day, New Night; 1974)

filmi   garish make-up or clothes (Hinglish)

formula film   a run-of-the-mill movie

item girl   a starlet with garish make-up and clothes who performs a five-minute sexy caberet number in a movie

item number   a raunchy song and dance number, which can involve anything from poles to waterfalls to come-hither gestures

kahani mein twist   Hinglish for 'a twist in the plot' – this describes surprise elements in the script, often a self-deprecating dialogue to explain seemingly strange, non sequitur goings on

multi-starrer   many stars appearing in one film

nahi chalegi   'the film will flop', literally 'won't walk' (Hindi)

paisa vasool   your money's worth (Hindi)

parallel cinema   the film movement of the 1970s which sought to provide an alternative to Bombay commercial cinema, largely funded by the state-run NFDC

picture chalegi   the movie will work (Hinglish)

playback singer   singers who sing the songs which actors lip-synch in films

side hero   a second-fiddle hero

talkies   cinema theatre, pronounced 'tal·kij' or 'ta·keez'

Technicolour   a colour film (company name)

In the past, filmmakers recycled common formulas in hit films. Traditional box-office successes often involved the story of two brothers lost during a crowded *mela* (festival) in childhood. This separated-siblings formula became known as *bichhde bhai* (Hindi for 'separated brothers').

The plotline usually has one growing up to become a cop, the other a villain thus setting the stage for confrontations and dramatic dialogues. The warring siblings are touchingly reunited in the last scene while jointly humming a lullaby mouthed by mum – who's by now blind or, at the very least, widowed. Examples of this fertile formula include *Yaadon Ki Baraat*, *Amar, Akbar, Anthony* and a zillion other Hindi films of the '70s and '80s.

Another favourite theme is the love story between two perfectly groomed people who not only belong to the opposite sex, but also to opposite sides of the track: one unfathomably rich, the other unspeakably poor. Sometimes the plot revolves around a love triangle where the choice is between a *lovematch* (fiancé(e) of choice) or the arranged fiancé(e).

Hindi films are currently moving away from these stereotypes and exploring nonromantic and more profound subject matter along with expanded linguistic horizons.

HOUSEHOLD NAMES: ENTERTAINERS

Aamir Khan (1965–)

Acted in and produced *Lagaan: Once Upon a Time in India* (2001), which was nominated in 2002 for the Academy Award for the best foreign language film. His first film as producer and writer/director, *Taare Zameen Par* (Hindi for 'stars on earth'; 2007), about a dyslexic child's world has won rave reviews from critics and audiences alike.

Aishwarya Rai (1973–)

Called the **Crossover Star**, the former Miss World has charmed audiences around the globe with her roles in *Bride and Prejudice* (2004) and *Provoked* (2006).

Ajit (1922–1998)

The late *villain* actor Hamid Ali Khan, whose stage name was Ajit, spawned a series of jokes in English lampooning his Punjabi accent and linguistic sensibilities. His molls Mona ('Mona, darling!') and Lilly ('Lilly, don't be silly!') featured alongside him.

Amitabh Bachchan (1942–)

The original **Angry Young Man**, this suave, age-defying superstar and winner of several awards, is still going strong with hit films featuring him in the lead role. He also hosted the highly successful Indian adaptation of the UK TV show *Who Wants To Be A Millionaire* (*Kaun Banega Crorepati* in Hindi – **KBC** for short).

Manoj Night Shyamalan (1970–)

This Indian-born US-based director provided cinematic chills for worldwide audiences with movies like *The Sixth Sense* and *The Village*.

Mira Nair (1957–)

The accomplished Indian-born director, writer and producer of award-winning films such as *Salaam Bombay! Mississippi Masala* and *Monsoon Wedding*.

>

Padma Lakshmi (1970–)
Acted in the Bollywood flop *Boom* (2003) before later resurfacing as author Salman Rushdie's third wife (now ex-wife) and a cooking-show host in Britain.

Shabana Azmi (1950–)
The diva of Indian acting, she propelled the art-house wave in mainstream cinema. Beginning with *Ankur* (The Bud; 1974), she's acted in many award-winning roles and is still going strong.

Shahrukh Khan (1965–)
This actor began his career on TV with the serial *Fauji* (Military Man) and went on to become the darling of the masses with super-duper hits like *Baazigar* (The Gambler; 1993) and *Kuch Kuch Hota Hai* (Something is Happening; 1998), and has more recently been celebrated for his role as hockey coach Kabir Khan in *Chak De! India* (2007) and his double role in home production *Om Shanti Om* (2007).

Shekhar Kapur (1945–)
His movie *Bandit Queen* (1994), which was based on controversial Indian bandit-turned-politician Phoolan Devi, made international headlines. He went on to make *Elizabeth* (1998) and *Elizabeth: The Golden Age* (2007), both starring Australian actress Cate Blanchett.

Television

When cable television exploded into Indian living rooms in the early 1990s, the massive audience became all of a sudden exposed to American English. The latest in American music, movies, clothes and news was instantly accessible. The cavalry charge of Western shows tend to make a belated arrival on Indian idiot boxes, so that when Indians gush over *Friends, Desperate Housewives, Frasier* or *Will and Grace*, they're likely to be talking about episodes from at least two seasons back (unless they've managed to get hold of pirated DVDs, which may be one season ahead).

The popular home-grown *K serials* – with titles starting with the supposedly auspicious letter *k* – are Hindi soap operas notorious for depicting women in an overly traditional manner. These women wear *sindoor* (red sacred powder) on their scalp, a *mangalsutra* (a necklace symbolising marriage) around their necks and *kanjivaram* (a heavy type of silk) saris. Their devotion to the men is complete through their pious observation of *Karva Chauth* (a fasting ceremony thought to increase a husband's longevity). Free of these kinds of traditional restraints are some of the detective serials like *Karamchand, CID* and *Jasoos Vijay*.

Theatre

From puppetry (*kathputhli ka khel*, Hindi for 'play by puppets') to modern existential dilemmas and street theatre, the Indian stage has seemingly been set forever. Mahesh Dattani, Alyque Padamsee and Girish Karnad are prominent names presently associated with this art form called *natak* ('drama' in Hindi). When it comes to drama these are some words you may find useful:

bhavai   folk theatre in Gujarat (Gujarati, from Sanksrit *bhava* 'emotion')

ekanki   a one-act play (Hindi)

jatra   folk theatre in Bengal (Bengali)

koodiyattam Sanskrit theatre tradition of Kerala (Malayalam)

nautanki a type of theatre in northern India, also used to suggest an overdramatised or fake situation (as in *What's this nautanki?*) (Hindi)

Ram-lila the story of **Lord Rama**, the *Ramayana*, enacted over 10 days leading up to the Hindu festival of Dussehra, when the effigy of the ten-headed demon king Ravana is burnt (Hindi)

ras-lila depicts the love story of Radha and **Lord Krishna** – performed in the Mathura region of Uttar Pradesh (Hindi)

Sanskrit theatre the oldest form of Indian theatre, dating back to 150 BC. Sudraka's *Mrichchakatika* (The Little Clay Cart) is an example of this theatrical style. The theatre principles set out in Bharata's *Natyashastra* (The Science of Drama) is a classic still studied by drama students.

sutradhar serves the purpose of a chorus in Greek classical theatre, but only involves a solo narrator who talks directly to the audience (Hindi)

tamasha folk theatre in Maharashtra

Music

From a *lori* (lullaby) to a funeral dirge, music has traditionally marked Indian milestones in chants and couplets from the cradle to the grave. From the cadences of a Sanskrit *shloka* (poem) to the latest **Sufic** (mystical Muslim) nuances, Indian lyricism assaults or soothes your ears depending on its decibel levels and how you like your tunes. Marriages, religious events and minifestivals, such as a child's naming ceremony, are all occasions for hiring a band. Most of what you hear will be film music (Bollywood style), so get ready to dance. Music with English vocals is increasingly popular among young listeners who play it at maximum volume through their loudspeakers, preferably in a public place. Traditional music is now relegated to formal concerts or state functions.

Clubs and cafés usually have TVs tuned to music channels like MTV or Channel V, with the volume muted. This provides a visual backdrop for the mismatched American rock or *Indi pop* (Indian pop music) booming through the interior. Plain and relatively discreet instrumental music is played in trains, hospitals and airplanes. If you can tune out the surrounding soundscape this can be great for relaxation. Instrumental music typically features the *sitar* (made famous by the legendary musician Pandit Ravi Shankar, who performed with The Beatles), the *ik-tara*, the *sarod*, the *sarangi* , the *tanpura* (all string instruments), the *pakhawaj* (drum), the *shehnai* (similar to an oboe), or the *tabla* or *dhol* (drums). Local music styles include the following:

antakshari   a game based on songs from movie soundtracks where players sings songs starting with the letter that the previous song ends with (from Hindi *ant* 'end' and *akshar* 'alphabet')

antara   verse (Hindi)

bhajan   Hindu devotional songs (Hindi)

Carnatic music   classical music from southern India (Indian English)

ENGLISH LYRICS

The entry of Western music into India was via the back door, when holidaymakers in the 1970s brought in ABBA and Boney M, making them more popular than Elvis Presley or The Beatles ever were in India. As far as English-language pop in India is concerned, there was no looking back after that. Soon Madonna and Michael Jackson ruled the airwaves before finally ceding to a new generation of Western pop artists. Whereas Western classical music remains a connoisseur's realm, Indian film music has been greatly influenced by popular Western beats.

Chitrahar a film-song show on Indian TV, the first of its kind in India – very popular before the arrival of cable TV (Hindi)

disc music a term referring to rave, techno, fusion and trance music

ghazal a form of Urdu poetry, which can be put to music. It was made popular by Jagjit Singh, Anup Jalota and many others. (Urdu)

Hindustani music a major type of Indian classical music from northern India (Indian English)

kavita poem (Hindi)

kirtan Hindu devotional songs (Hindi)

mukhda chorus (Hindi)

mushaira a poetry reading (Urdu)

qawwali the devotional music of the Sufi Muslims accompanied by clapping, brought into the global limelight by the late Pakistani ***qawwal*** (***qawwali*** singer) Nusrat Fateh Ali Khan (Urdu)

shaayari poetry (Urdu)

sher couplet (Urdu)

sur a note (Hindi)

taal the beat or rhythm (Hindi)

Bollywood music is big business in India as the majority of movies are musicals. From the use of Hinglish lyrics such as **Meri pant bhi sexy** (My pants are sexy too), there are now unapologetic English lyrics exhorting you to ***just chill***.

The Hollywood hit *Moulin Rouge!* (2001), directed by Baz Luhrmann, used Bollywood music, including the song *Chhamma-Chhamma* from the Hindi movie *China Gate*. Diaspora music by ***desi*** (Indian) immigrants in the US has contributed the following items to Indian English vocabulary:

curry rock   the immigrant experience told
musically by US East Coast geeks

geeksta rap   music glamourising the pursuit
of science and technology

H1-Bees   a *desi* (Indian) band of techies who sing the
blues (a pun on the H-1B visa for guest
workers in the US)

HOUSEHOLD NAMES: MUSIC

Freddie Mercury (1946–1991)
Born Farrokh Bulsara, this Parsi from Mumbai was the lead singer in the band Queen prior to his death in 1991. He's still remembered for a number of hits including *Radio Ga Ga*, *Crazy Little Thing Called Love* and *Bohemian Rhapsody*.

AR Rahman (1966–)
Rahman composed the music for several films in Tamil and Hindi, most of which are top hits on everyone's lips. He also composed music for Andrew Lloyd Webber's Broadway show *Bombay Dreams*.

KJ Yesudas (1940–)
Mainly a Malayali singer, he figured in the charts from the 1970s to the 1990s with film music as well as devotional songs. His interpretation of the *Carnatic* (South Indian classical music) style of singing has given him long-lasting celebrity.

Asha Bhosle (1933–)
From seductive rasps to baby lisps, she can do them all. A famous *playback singer* recording some of Bollywood's biggest hits, she has also teamed up with several Western artists, Boy George notable among them.

MS Subbulakshmi (1916–2004)
Known as the Nightingale of India, this exceptional singer enthralled the world with her mastery over *Carnatic* nuances.

Dance

Never shy to shake a leg, Indians can choose from a rich treasure chest of traditional and modern dances. Known as *Naach* in Hindi or *Nritya* in Sanskrit, dance has waltzed into Indian English with myriad folk forms such as *Kathakali* (a southern-Indian dance-drama), *Bharatnatyam* (Bharat's dance), *kathak* (a northern-Indian dance form), *mohiniyattam* (a classical dance from Kerala), *odissi* (classical dance from Orissa) and *kuchipudi* (a classical dance from Andhra Pradesh). Other dance forms include:

bhangra a Punjabi harvest or thanksgiving dance, punctuated with cries of *balle-balle* (hurrah) as dancers raise colourful handkerchiefs and nod their heads, attired in equally colourful turbans, to herald the spring (Punjabi)

Chhau a tribal martial dance form from the east of India (Oriya)

jazz-dancing a highly individualistic fusion of Western dance forms

kai-kotti kali a hand-clapping dance by Kerala women wearing gold-bordered saris of white cotton – usually performed during the Onam festival (from Malayalam *kai* 'hand', *kotti* 'clap' and *kali* 'play')

mujra a courtesan's dance with mostly Urdu poetry or songs, which originated in *kothas* (brothels) (Urdu)

tandav the dance of Lord Shiva (Sanskrit)

Parties

With *hijras* (sari-clad eunuchs) invading every family celebration with their characteristic flat-palmed claps, loudspeakers blaring religious songs, and enough food to make a fasting Hindu cry, the Indian party scene is an extraordinary sensory experience. Whether it's a festival or funeral, Indians are experts at marking an occasion. The extended family system means weekend get-togethers turn into parties by default. In northern India you may be invited to a *party-sharty*, a *bash* or *gaana-bajaana* (Hindi for 'song-dance').

At Indian weddings the menu is as elaborate as the bridal sari, though modernists are increasingly opting for the more convenient buffets or a simple *biryani* (a fragrant rice casserole). Food can be *hot and spicy* (good) or *boring* (bland). Up north, a typical wedding lasts for days and entails a lawn littered with food stalls offering freshly made *tandoori rotis*, *kebabs*, *fruit-chaats* (fruit salads) and multiple *mithai* (sweets). Most Hindu weddings in the south serve only vegetarian fare to preserve the purity of the occasion. Traditionally, gender dictates who you hang out with on the big day. Men and women split up forming separate groups. That way both groups can let their hair down without inhibitions.

Other popular parties include *kitty parties* (a social event for bored Indian housewives), *tambola* (a number game) and *taash* (card) parties where rummy and gin fuel the recreational gambling. *Diwali* (the Hindu Festival of the Lamps) celebrations, weddings and other functions are often preceded by these card parties. As in the West *chit-chat*, *small-small talk* and *PC* (polite conversation) lubricate the proceedings. If someone invites you to a *bachcha* (kids) *party* don't forget your earplugs – the kids are always loud.

happy birthday party	a birthday bash
rocking, man	New Age lingo for 'I'm having a good time'
shosha	showy or gaudy
treat	slang for 'party', eg *you owe us a treat for your promotion*

Gambling

Satta is a form of local gambling on almost anything from election results to the outcome of cricket matches. Betting on *taash* (cards) is the core of most betting games. Entire industries are devoted to helping people gamble on the cricket and horses. In cities, it is *tambola* (a numbers game) that delights, despite being played for paltry stakes. In Mumbai, *matka* is all the rage for gambling addicts who have a yen to test their luck by pulling out numbered slips from an earthen pot. If there is a good thing about gambling in India, it's that there is always a human element and, so far, slot machines have made few incursions into Indian life.

Festivals

There is only one way to put on a festival in India and that is with supreme zeal. Travel the country for a thousand years and you will never come across a half-hearted celebration.

The festive season kicks off every year with the military themed *Republic Day Festival* held on 26 January. In Delhi, Republic Day celebrations feature processions with floats bearing aesthetically arranged *jhankis* (displays of each state's specialties and innovations).

The main Hindu festivals like *Diwali* (the Festival of the Lamps), *Dussehra* (a festival celebrating the triumph of good over evil following the defeat of the Buffalo Demon by the warrior goddess Durga), *Janmashtami* (the anniversary of Lord Krishna's birth), and *Holi* (a harvest festival where people drench each other with colour), all keep company with a whole host of regional religious celebrations, mourning rituals and everything in between, some of which are given below:

Baisakhi   Sikhs commemorate the founding of the Khalsa order by Guru Gobind Singh in the month of Vaisakh (roughly April) in the Sikh calendar

Christmas Christians celebrate the anniversary of the birth of Jesus Christ on 25 December

Durga Puja a five-day Bengali festival for the goddess Mother Durga, culminating in the celebration of *Dussehra* (see box p82)

Easter this Christian holiday marks the crucifixion and resurrection of Christ

Ganesh Chaturthi to mark the birthday of the elephant god Ganesa, life-like clay models of him are decorated and offerings are made of red flowers, coconut, jaggery, *modakas* (rice-flour sweets) and *rakta chandan* (red unguent). It is usually held in early September.

Holi revelries involve the use of make-up in vibrant colours, both liquid and powder, called *gulal*. Celebrants, usually garbed in white, smear each other with colours, crying, *Holi hai!* (it's Holi!). *Bhang pakoras* (salty snacks laced with cannabis) and *thandai* (a milky drink laced with intoxicants) are served.

Karva Chauth women fasting for their husbands' longevity decorate special sacred offering plates, called *puja thali*, with coconut, sweets and religious objects and eat only after the full moon has risen in the Hindu month of Kartik (roughly February/March)

SWINGING SIXTY

Shashtipoorthi is the Hindu celebration of a sixtieth birthday. With great pomp and ceremony, the children and relatives of the sexagenarian celebrate this important milestone. The word comes from Sanskrit *shashti* 'sixty' and *poorthi* 'complete'.

Lodi this harvest festival, held towards the end of January, sees people dance energetically around a bonfire and make offerings of peanuts, popcorn and *revdi* (a sweet made of sesame seeds and sugar) by flinging them into the fire. The fire represents the old year, burnt away, to make way for the new.

Mahavir Jayanti this Jain festival held in the Hindu month of Chaitra commemorates the birth of Mahavira – the founder of Jainism (from sanskrit *jayanti* 'anniversary')

Martyr's Day this holiday is observed on 30 January to commemorate the day in 1948 when Mahatma Gandhi was assassinated

Navroz the Parsi New Year, held in August

Navratri this Hindu festival is held on the nine nights leading up to *Dussehra*. During this time Hindus take part in rituals, fasting, prayer and folk dancing after sundown. (From Sanskrit *nava* 'nine' and *ratri* 'night'.)

Onam a boisterous snake-boat race in Kerala's Alapuzha district heralds this harvest festival in August or September with *pookalam* patterns (floral designs using freshly plucked flowers) outside front doors and a vegetarian *sadhya* (feast) served on plantain leaves

Pongal a four-day harvest festival celebrated in Tamil Nadu in the south with colourful *kolams* (elaborate drawings) placed outside front doors to attract Lady Luck. Colourfully decorated cattle with bells around their necks are paraded through the streets.

Raksha Bandhan a symbolic ritual to strengthen sibling ties. During this ritual sisters tie decorative bracelets on their brothers' wrists, whereby the brothers promise to look after their sisters forever. This festival is usually celebrated on the full moon in Shraavana (August). (From Hindi *raksha* 'protection' and *bandhan* 'bond'.)

Slightly less formal festivities include:

Goan Carnival this carnival, a hangover from Goa's Portuguese past, is usually held in February. A *King Momo* is selected who presides over the three-day cultural festivities that include street plays, songs and dances.

Kumbh Mela a Hindu religious pilgrimage that's held four times in every twelve years. The exact date of a Kumbh Mela is astrologically determined.

Makar Sankranti a kite-flying festival held in Gujarat and other parts of northern India. The sky is ablaze with myriad colours and paper designs dipping and soaring. It is traditionally celebrated before mid-January.

Nauchandi ka Mela essentially a large fair, this event is held on the second Sunday after *Holi* in Meerut in Uttar Pradesh. It's a merry carousel of eats, rides, brightly coloured bangles and sales of *dupatta* (lengths of cotton draped across the shoulders). (From Hindi *nau* 'nine', *chand* 'moon' and *mela* 'carnival'.)

Thrissur Pooram called 'The Festival of Festivals', it's held centre-stage in the Vadakkunnatha temple of the Thrissur district of Kerala in the Malayalam month of Medam (May). A highlight of the festivals is a procession by two rows of 13 richly decorated elephants, each carrying an ornate parasol holder, a peacock-fan carrier and a yak-tail fly-whisk wielder. Percussion and wind orchestras play until sunset when fireworks explode in the sky. (From Malayalam *pooram* 'festival'.)

Shopping

Accompanying the rise of India's middle class are, maybe not surprisingly, thousands of advertisements exhorting consumers to shop till they drop. In the last couple of years, credit card usage has skyrocketed.

Suburban malls provide air-conditioned refuge from the city streets. Noisy brats can be dumped in arcade game rooms while the adults roam free, window-shopping and boutique-hopping. Visual displays large on wow-factor do a good job of enticing customers into the *dukaan* (Hindi for 'shop'). India, especially in the north, is a shopping mecca where *export rejects*, *chappals* (sandals) and handbags can be picked up cheap if you know how to bargain. Here is some one-size-fits-all haggle talk for your next Indian shopping adventure:

bumper sale	an annual or mega sale (Indian English)
discount hai	discounted (Hinglish, literally 'there is a discount')
ek ka do	a sales tactic where you get a second item free with the first (Hindi, literally 'one for two')
factory sale	a sale at factory or wholesale prices (Indian English)
sale ka maal	goods for sale (Hinglish from Hindi *maal* 'goods' and *ka* 'for')
sasta maal	cheap goods (Hindi)

Colourful colloquial expressions permeate every aspect of Indian culture. For example, the colour red is used in a number of intriguing colloquialisms. When cooking, onions should be *reddened* (made *lal* 'red') but the Hindi word for red *lal* is also what a mother calls her darling child. If you're enraged you'll be *red with anger* – following an analogy with a Hindi expression that uses *lal* 'red' to describe anger. If you're slightly less maddened, you could be *red-yellow* (from Hindi *lal-pila*).

However, red isn't the only way that anger can be described in India. If you're starting to see red, you can also be described as being *inside anger* (a literal translation of the Hindi *gusse mein*) or *bubbling with fire* (from Hindi *aag baboola*). If you're merely feeling irritated, your *brains are fried*.

Describing people

A male can be referred to as *our man*, *uncle*, *charlie*, *chappie*, *bugger*, *banda*, *janab*, *Johnny*, *the joker* or just *so-and-so*. He might also be *kadka* (broke), *khaddoos* (short-tempered), *kanjoos* (miserly), *khoosat* (elderly) or *maha khush* (very happy).

Meanwhile a woman can be *bindaas* (a carefree babe), *homely* (home-loving), a *city-girl* or *cheapda* (sluttish). You can call people you know a *yaar* (friend), a *jigri dost* (bosom buddy), *langotiya yaar* (loin-cloth pal) or even a *chaddi-dost* (underwear friend) – the latter goes back to a Hindi expression meaning a pal from the time you were in nappies.

Here are some more slang expressions that will help you describe people and make friends in India:

ABCD	American Born Confused Desi – young Americans of Indian origin (Hinglish, from Hindi *des* 'country')
awara	a vagabond (Hindi)
B	short for 'bitch' – as in *she's a real B* (Indian English)
bandar	ugly or stupid (Hindi for 'monkey')
bekaar	a useless or jobless person (Hindi)
BTM	stands for *behanji-turned-mod* – someone trying to be fashionable, but not succeeding (Hinglish, from Hindi *behenji* 'sister', slang for 'dowdy woman')

bhik-manga	a poor-looking person or someone who wants a loan (Hindi for 'beggar')
bechara	Hindi for 'poor thing'
chamcha	a sycophant (Hindi)
chaalu	an immoral girl (see also *fast* below) (Hindi)
chhakka	eunuch, also a wide-ranging derogatory term for effeminate men (Hindi slang)
crackpot	an idiot (Indian English)
dingo	a derogatory reference to an Anglo-Indian person (Indian English)
dandruff	a person who 'flakes out' and ditches their friends (Indian English)

fast	a word used to describe an immoral woman (Indian English)
goonda	a robber or hooligan (Hindi)
hijra	eunuch (Hindi)
ikka	a winner (Hindi for 'one')
jammer	someone who *jams up* (holds up) any type of proceedings (Indian English)
jungli	uncouth (Hindi for 'from the jungle')
kaala kaluta	dark-skinned (Hindi)
keep	a mistress (Indian English)
lafanga	a layabout (Hindi)
madrasi	a term for a South Indian, used by North Indians (from Madras, now called Chennai, a city in Tamil Nadu)
mawali	riffraff (Hindi)
maal	a well-endowed girl (Hindi for 'the goods')
mona	a Sikh who does not grow his hair; also called *cut Sard*
motu	a fatso (Hindi)
northie	a North Indian (Indian English)
patlu	skinny (Hindi)
Poo	selfish, affected – after the character Poo in the movie *Kabhi Kushi Kabhi Gam…* (Sometimes Happiness, Sometimes Sorrow)
rangeela	a fun person (Hindi for 'colourful')
ringtone DJ	an annoying person who incessantly shuffles through mobile-phone ringtones (Indian English)
Sardar	a title used for Sikh men (Hindi)
society lady	a socialite (Indian English)
southie	a south Indian (Indian English)
Soorma Bhopali	a man wearing kohl eyeliner, also used to refer to a character in a film named after the city Bhopal and Hindi *soorma* 'kohl'

stepney	a spare tyre, also slang for a mistress (Indian English, originally from Stepney Tyre & Rubber Co Ltd)
short circuit	quick temper, eg *He has a short circuit* (Indian English)
Surdas	blind – refers to the name of a famous blind Hindi poet – as in *don't be a Surdas* (don't be short-sighted)
tapori	a street-wise guy (Mumbai Hindi)
totla	a lisper or stutterer (Hindi)
total pagal	totally mad (Hinglish, from Hindi *pagal* 'mad')
VVIP	a very-very important person, usually a politician (Indian English)

Put-downs

A part of being polite is, of course, knowing what not to say. So, even though you shouldn't have much cause to use them in practice, the following Indian English put-downs are good to be aware of.

a real cartoon	no reference to any animated character, but slang for 'idiot'
as if!	dismissal, eg 'He told me he was going to London to meet the queen' – 'As if!'

give it back	get even, retaliate or take revenge, eg *he shouted, but I gave it back to him*
give it to him	get physically or verbally violent, eg *give it to him left and right*
rascal	a common southern insult, with stress on the *r*
show-offing	potential rivals who 'show off' (brag/boast) are 'show-offs' who 'do the *show-offing*'
tight slap	painful slap, eg *I'll give you one tight slap!*
what-what?	meant to intimidate, eg in response to a threat or insult
what he thinks of himself?	rhetorical query about an adversary

Actions

Indian English is rich in slang for actions, derived from standard English and the many languages of India. Hinglish coinings are apt to lend more colour to an action, eg *giving gaalis* (from Hindi *gaali* 'curse') is to curse freely and *phenkofying* ('throwing' from Hindi *phenk* 'throw') is slang for bluffing.

aunty is visiting	slang for a woman having her period (Indian English)
bhaanda fodna	to explode a myth or uncover a lie (Hindi)

GROOVY GOOLIES

Not only has Hindi contributed heavily to Indian English slang, but its influence has reached as far as the beaches of Australia. If you hear an Aussie cricket player double over in pain and yell out 'He got me in the *goolies*', then he's probably taken a fast bowl to his nether regions. Goolies originally comes from the Hindustani word *goli*, which means 'ball' or 'bullet'.

chadaofy	to flatter someone, to egg someone on (from Hindi *chadna* 'climb')
chutiya banana	an offensive expression meaning 'make a fool of' (from Hindi *chut* 'female genitals' and *banana* 'make')
choona lagana	literally 'to whitewash', it is slang for 'to trick someone' (from Hindi *choona* 'slaked lime' and *lagana* 'put')
cut le	leave in a hurry/stealthily (Hinglish, from English *cut* and Hindi *le* 'take')
don't maaro cool effect	don't show off (Hinglish, from Hindi *maar* 'hit, affect')
gag on to something	catch on to something
they were nabbed	they got caught/arrested
make kachra	to spoil something (from Hindi *kachra* 'garbage')
ragdoed	made to work hard (Hinglish, from Hindi *ragad* 'rub against')
ragged	a victim of college ragging (known as 'hazing' in American English)
rattoed	learned by rote (Hinglish, from Hindi *ratta* 'memorise')
under-standing	to be standing underneath

JAIL JARGON

In 2002, the Indian journalist Ifthikar Geelani was falsely accused of spying for *ISI* (the Pakistani Intelligence Agency). He was jailed for seven months. Geelani wrote about his experiences of being held in a police lockup in his chilling book *My Days In Prison*. His depiction of life behind bars included the prison slang *Tata Sumo driving* (hauling garbage) and *Gandhi* (Rs 500 note).

Other slang

Every corner of India rings with vernacular translations, folk-tale morals and such unique fusions of words that the ear has enough exercise trying to decode one slang expression from another.

ajeeb	weird (Hindi)
compounder	a person manning a medicine counter; a quack (doctor)
dhaansu	another word for 'wow' when describing something, eg *very dhaansu music* (Hindi)
elephant's teeth	something that's largely ornamental or showy (from the Hindi saying 'an elephant has separate teeth for eating and showing')
high end	of very high quality; often used sarcastically of work and people
khandani	classy; of good breeding or parentage (Hindi)
LIC	the acronym for Life Insurance Corporation now stands for any insurance policy
ML	a moral lecture or a mother-in-law
MMS	multimedia messaging – slang for covert camera footage of celebrities caught in compromising situations
naya paisa	a new kid on the block, literally 'new paisa (unit of currency)' (Hindi)
OTT	over the top, especially in dress sense
Peter	a speaker of fluent English (Indian English, used in Tamil Nadu)

Acronyms

Indians love their acronyms almost as much as the British love civil service. Below are some acronyms commonly used in India:

ASSOCHAM	Associated Chambers of Commerce
BJP	Bharatiya Janata Party (Hindu nationalist party)
BSE	Bombay Stock Exchange
BSF	Border Security Force
CBI	Central Bureau of Investigation
CGHS	Central Government Health Scheme
CII	Confederation of Indian Industry
CPM	Communist Party of India (Marxist)
CVC	Central Vigilance Commission (the commission set up to receive complaintsabout corruption and abuse of power)
FICCI	Federation of Indian Chambers of Commerce and Industry
FII	foreign institutional investors
FOC	free of charge
IAS	Indian Administrative Service
IFS	Indian Foreign Service
IMFL	Indian-made foreign liquor (liquor which is consumed by the upper and middle classes in India as distinct from *country liquor*)
IPS	Indian Police Service
LoC	line of control in Kashmir between India and Pakistan
NDA	National Democratic Alliance (the coalition between the Bharatiya

	Janata Party and a number of other parties)
OBC	Other Backward Classes – an official term for castes or communities that are identified as socially and educationally disadvantaged
ONGC	Oil and Natural Gas Corporation
PD	punishment detail
RBI	Reserve Bank of India
SAARC	South Asian Association for Regional Cooperation
SC	Supreme Court, the highest court in the land
SEBI	Securities and Exchange Board of India
SI	a subinspector of police
UPA	United Progressive Alliance, a political coalition
ULFA	United Liberation Front of Asom, the rebel outfit seeking independence for Assam in northeast India

Abbreviations

Indians have a penchant for abbreviations. On university campuses across the country, it pays to know the difference between being a *despo* and a *fundoo*.

abs	absolutely
agro	agricultural
aggro	aggressive
arbit	arbitrary
despo	desperate (usually in unrequited love)
enthu	enthusiastic
expo	exposition
expi	expensive

fab	fabulous
fundas	fundamentals
fundoo	a fun guy
Gujju	a Gujarati
hospi	a hospital
hyper	hyper-sensitive
lab ass	a laboratory assistant
lech	lecherous
mixi	a food grinder
mod	modern
princi	principal
pross	a prostitute
pseud	pseudo
retro	retrograde
senti	sentimental
trad	traditional
ticks	tickets

MISUNDERSTANDINGS

Indian English wouldn't be half as fun without all its attendant misunderstandings, misinterpretations, and mispronunciations (at least to the ears of speakers of other varieties of English). Even the most finely adapted foreign ears will be baffled at some point. Popular Hindi phrases sound like familiar, but somehow indecipherable sentences in English. And speakers of Indian English can sometimes apply well-worn colloquialisms, recognised throughout the English-speaking world, somewhat differently. In India, *I am feeling hot* is not about sexual arousal but room temperature, *I like it hot* explains nothing more sordid than a penchant for spicy food, and if *someone is hot* then they are merely popular.

Misheard

In India, where hundreds of languages are striving to be heard, there are plenty of words that sound like standard English but have very different meanings. For example, in Hindi a 'duck' is a *battakh* and shouldn't be confused with one's derrière. If someone suggests you shave your *daadi*, they are referring to your beard, not your trusty ol' pa.

The Urdu *yakeen* (trust) sounds suspiciously like 'yukky' or 'you're keen.' When offered a *phookat* trip, it means you can travel for 'free', not to Thailand's Phuket.

You say what?

If you hear someone say they have a *two-in-one*, you might be tempted to ask 'a two-in-one what?' But don't worry, here is some vocabulary to help you out. These are some Indian English words which sound misleadingly familiar, but which are actually not used at all or used differently in other varieties of English.

barber	hairdresser
bearer	waiter
bank clerk	bank cashier
bed sheet	bed sheets or bed covers
buttocks	bottom
curd	yogurt
curtains	blinds
cool drink	soft drink
cooling glasses	sun glasses
godown	warehouse
government holiday	public holiday
ground floor	first floor (American English)
knicker	boy's shorts
latrine	toilet
light	electric power
lime	lemon or lime
lokus	locals
nose cut	humiliation
nosy	snot, nasal mucus
package	parcel
prepone	advance, reschedule forward
parcel	takeaway
rag-picker	homeless child who makes a living picking up paper scraps from the streets
sweetmeats	sweets, lollies
swimming dress	swimming costume

tight	broke
tomato sauce	ketchup (American English)
two-in-one	boom box
veg	vegan
down-down	is an attempt to decry someone's worthlessness, like when a team is losing
really-really	underlines the veracity of a story, eg *He really-really prayed*
tooth powder	toothpaste in powder form

Hindi sayings

Some of Hindi's best sayings make absolutely no sense whatsoever when translated directly into English, which doesn't stop Hindi speakers from frequently doing just that. Here are some classic Hindi phrases along with their literal and implied meanings.

aage-peechhe koi nahi   (Literally: 'no-one ahead or behind') no-one cares for you and you have no-one to care for

aam ke aam, guthliyon ke daam   (Literally: 'mango for mango and money for seeds') not only do you get the mango, you get money for the seed, implying a double benefit

bagal mein chhuri, munh mein Ram-Ram   (Literally: 'knife in armpit, Lord Rama on lips') someone who piously chants Lord Rama's name but carries a knife to harm others, implying a hypocrite

bandar kya jaane adrak ka swad? (Literally: 'what does a monkey know of the taste of ginger?') said of someone with no expertise in a given area

char chand lagana (Literally: 'to add four moons') to enhance the beauty of something

char log kya kahenge? (Literally: 'what will four people say?') what will others say?

chhati pe saanp lotna (Literally: 'to have snakes crawling on one's chest') to seethe with jealousy

dhal mein kuchh kala (Literally: 'there's something black in the lentil soup') something suspicious is going on

ghode bech ke sona (Literally: 'to sleep after selling your horses') to sleep soundly

kaanon mein joon tak nahi rengi (Literally: 'not even a tiny louse crawled into his ear') implying the person paid no heed

lohe ke chane chabana (Literally: 'to chew chickpeas of iron') to be toughened, prepared to face severe tests

laaton ke bhoot baaton se nahi mante (Literally: 'those who are long accustomed to kicks will not respond to words') get tough with toughies

naach na jaane, angan tedha (Literally: 'doesn't know the dance but blames the crooked floor') said of people who give excuses for their lack of expertise

The languages of India

With hundreds of native languages, the linguistic array found in India is dazzling, not to mention astounding, bamboozling and utterly overwhelming. At the tip of the iceberg are the 22 languages recognised by the Constitution – Assamese, Bengali, Bodo, Dogri, Gujarati, Hindi, Kannada, Kashmiri, Konkani, Maithili, Malayalam, Manipuri, Marathi, Nepali, Oriya, Punjabi, Sanskrit, Santhali, Sindhi, Tamil, Telugu and Urdu. Each state uses one or more of these official languages – Assam, for example, functions in Assamese and Bodo. Each of the official languages is described briefly in this section.

Other languages are spoken by large populations, but aren't ranked as 'official' languages. And sometimes it's hard to tell where one language starts and another begins – Hindi, the national language spoken by around 400 million Indians, actually comprises a number of distinct languages and dialects – so what does your Varanasi taxi driver speak? How exactly did a country of more than a billion people end up speaking over 1600 dialects or 'mother tongues'?

INDO-ARYAN LANGUAGES

The two major language families in India are Indo-Aryan and Dravidian. Indo-Aryan is the most spoken language family in India, now famously incarnated as Hindi and Urdu, with another 200 related variants. Sanskrit is the oldest recorded of these languages and is found in the sacred literature of

Official languages of India

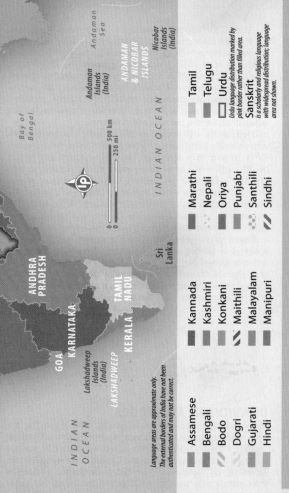

Official languages of India

INDIAN OCEAN

Bay of Bengal

Andaman Sea

Andaman Islands (India)

Nicobar Islands (India)

ANDAMAN & NICOBAR ISLANDS

ANDHRA PRADESH

GOA

KARNATAKA

KERALA

TAMIL NADU

Lakshadweep Islands (India)

LAKSHADWEEP

Sri Lanka

INDIAN OCEAN

0   500 km
0   250 mi

Language areas are approximate only.
The external borders of India have not been
authenticated and may not be correct.

- Assamese
- Bengali
- Bodo
- Dogri
- Gujarati
- Hindi

- Kannada
- Kashmiri
- Konkani
- Maithili
- Malayalam
- Manipuri

- Marathi
- Nepali
- Oriya
- Punjabi
- Santhili
- Sindhi

- Tamil
- Telugu
- Urdu

*Urdu language distribution marked by
pink border rather than filled area.*

Sanskrit
*is a scholarly and religious language
with widespread distribution; language
area not shown.*

171

the Vedas, the canon of Hinduism. The related languages, the Prakrits, developed into several literary languages. One famous descendent is Pali, the liturgical language of Theravada Buddhism across Asia, written in various scripts. The Prakrit language used to write Jain scriptures, known as Ardhamagadhi, was an archaic form of Magadhi (currently spoken by over 10 million people predominantly in Bihar). Maharashtri, probably the most widespread of the Prakrits, was used to write Ancient Indian drama and is the ancestor of Marathi.

The Prakrits, also known as Middle Indic languages, were subsequently transformed by the Muslim invasions between the 13th and 16th centuries. Farsi (also known as Persian) became influential, to be taken over by Urdu as the language of power in Delhi. Simultaneously, Urdu's variant Deccani was born in South India – now known as Dakhni, it's spoken by Muslims on the continent's Deccan plateau. Sindhi, spoken in Gujarat and Rajasthan, was a popular language for Sufi poetry between the 14th and 18th centuries. Sometimes considered a dialect of Punjabi, the Dogri language has 2 millions speakers in Jammu and Kashmir and surrounding areas and is distinguished by its tones, an unusual trait for a language of this family. Maithili was traditionally the speech of Mithila, a kingdom of Ancient India named in the *Ramayana* (see box p70); today it's spoken by 20 million people in Bihar.

DRAVIDIAN LANGUAGES
Legends related to Dravidian languages often claim that the language itself originated in a vast, ancient continent far to the south – a theory which sounds as well supported as various attempts by linguists to relate the Dravidian family to Finnish, Japanese or Australian Aboriginal languages. Whatever their history may be, the languages in this group are today

mostly spoken in South India. Tamil is the classical Southern Dravidian tongue, with the oldest recorded literature in the Dravidian languages dating from the 3rd century BC. A lesser known relative is Tulu, spoken by nearly two million people in Karnataka and Kerala. The Gondi language of Central India, with around two million speakers, has a rich folk literature in the form of both poetry and prose. In the northeastern states, the Kurukh language is spoken by some two million people yet is considered to be endangered because of the low literacy levels of its speakers. Both Gondi and Kurukh are isolated examples of the survival of Dravidian languages in the subcontinent's north. The hybrid Arwi tongue – a combination of Tamil and Arabic which was spoken by the Muslims of Tamil Nadu and Sri Lanka – is considered extinct in India.

AUSTRO-ASIATIC LANGUAGES

While the majority of India's languages have Indo-Aryan or Dravidian roots, you'll also hear Austro-Asiatic and Tibeto-Burmese languages spoken. Austro-Asiatic languages are generally believed to be the original languages of the east of India, subsequently influenced by incoming communities. India's most widely used language from this family is Santali, with official status in the country and around six million speakers in the northeastern states. It belongs to the Munda branch, just like the Korku language, which is spoken by less than 500,000 members of a little-known tribe in Madhya Pradesh and Maharashtra. The Nicobar Islands are home to 20,000 indigenous Nicobarese speakers. The six Nicobarese languages are often considered a separate branch within the Austro-Asiatic language family, although they show similarities with the Mon-Khmer languages of Southeast Asia.

TIBETO-BURMAN LANGUAGES

The original home of the Tibeto-Burman languages seems to have been the present-day China. The history of this language family in India is unclear, but around 60 of its languages are spoken today in the northern reaches of Indian territory. Tibetan, spoken by some 120,000 people, is a relative newcomer since the influx of Tibetan refugees which followed China's takeover of their homeland in 1949. Garo, the majority language of the people of the Garo Hills of Meghalaya, is closely related to Bodo, the language of Assam. Unlike most Indian languages, Garo uses the Roman alphabet as it lacks a written tradition of its own. Manipuri (also known as Meitei) is the lingua franca of the northeastern state of Manipuri; among its 1.2 million speakers there's a movement to return to their traditional Meitei Mayek script, instead of the Bengali script currently used. Kok Borok, the state language of Tripura, was first recorded in the Koloma script in the 1st century AD. The Ao language is spoken by some 140,000 residents of Nagaland; it has a rich legacy of folk tales, but with the increase in literacy the oral traditions are dying out. Mizo is the language of more than 500,000 people from the mountainous regions of northwestern India.

AND STILL MORE...

Aside from these major language groups, there are, of course, quirky anomalies. Unexpected but true, the Romani language spoken by the Roma people in Europe is related to Sanskrit, while the nearly extinct Khamyang language spoken by the small tribe of the same name in Assam and Arunachal Pradesh is related to Thai. India can also boast its very own language isolate – the Nihali language, spoken by some 5000 people in Madhya Pradesh and Maharashtra.

The Indian subcontinent was also the birthplace of several pidgins and creoles. Some of these are believed to be extinct today (such as a Portuguese-based creole in Goa), while others are still found – for example, the English-based Madras Pidgin in the south, used during the British rule, or the Hindi-based Bazaar Hindustani, spoken in the cities in northern India.

This awesome linguistic richness is just another factor in India's uniqueness.

Official languages of India

In this section, a glimpse is provided of each of the 22 official languages of India (apart from English, of course).

ASSAMESE

Despite being related to other languages of northern India, most closely to Bengali, Assamese (অসমীয়া ak·so·mee·a) is a distinctly non-Indian-sounding language: it has none of the peculiar rhotic-flavoured (r-sounding) consonants of many other Indian languages. This is due to contact with languages of Southeast Asia. Assamese, spoken by around 13 million people in India (mostly in the state of Assam), is a member of the Indo-European family's Indo-Aryan branch, therefore distantly related to the languages of Europe. Assamese was one of the languages used to write the *Charyapadas*, the mysterious millennium-old palm-leaf manuscripts containing Buddhist songs. It's written in Assamese script, which is similar to the script used to write Bengali. The British forced the people of Assam to use Bengali in the colonial times of the early 1800s – however, due to fierce opposition from the locals, they reinstated Assamese as the main official language a half-century later. Try your hand (or rather tongue) at this language – this will surely endear you to its proud owners!

Hello./Goodbye.	নমস্কাৰ। / বিদায়।	no·mos·kaar/bi·đai
Please.	অনুগ্ৰহ কৰি।	a·nu·gro·ha ko·ri
Thank you.	ধন্যবাদ।	đ'on·yo·baađ
Yes./No.	হয়। / নহয়।	hoy/no·hoy
Excuse me. (to get past/ to get attention)	ক্ষমা কৰিবে।	k'yo·ma ko·ri·bo
Sorry.	মই দুঃখিত।	moy duk·k'i·ta

Do you speak English?
আপুনি ইংৰাজি
ভাষা কব পাৰেনে ?
aa·pu·ni ing·ra·ji
b'a·k'a ko·bo paa·re·ne
I don't understand.
মই বুজি নাপাওঁ।
moy bu·ji na·pow

BENGALI

Bengali (বাংলা *bang*·la) is spoken by approximately 220 million people, ranking it in the top ten most spoken languages in the world. As well as being the official language of Bangladesh and the Indian states of Tripura and West Bengal, it's also spoken by large communities in North America and parts of Europe and the Middle East. Bengali belongs to the Indic group of the Indo-European language family, with Sanskrit, Hindi, Assamese and Oriya as close relatives.

Old Bengali, with its distinctive Brahmi script, had developed by about 1000AD and was strongly flavoured with Prakrit and Sanskrit words, to be spiced up with Farsi, Arabic and Turkish vocabulary when Bengal was conquered by Muslims in the 12th century AD. Today's Bengali has two literary forms – Shadhubhasha সাধুভাষা (lit: elegant language), the traditional literary style of 16th-century Middle Bengali, and Choltibhasha চলতি ভাষা (lit: running language), a more colloquial form based on the Bengali spoken in Kolkata.

The following are a few essentials in Bengali:

Hello (Hindu).	নমস্কার।	*no*·mohsh·kar
Hello (Muslim).	আস্সালাম	as·*sa*·lam
	ওয়ালাইকুম।	wa·*lai*·kum
Goodbye (Hindu).	নমস্কার।	*no*·mosh·kar
Goodbye (Muslim).	আল্লাহ্ হাফেজ়।	al·laa ha·fez
Please.	প্লিজ়।	pleez
Thank you.	ধন্যবাদ।	d'oh·noh·baad
Yes.	হ্যাঁ।	hang
No.	না।	naa
Excuse me.	শুনুন।	*shu*·nun
Sorry.	সরি।	*so*·ri
Help!	বাচান!	ba·cha·o

Do you speak (English)?
আপনি কি (ইংরেজি)   *aap*·ni ki (ing·*re*·ji)
বলত পারেন?   *bohl*·țe paa·ren
I don't understand.
না, আমি বুঝত পারছি না।   na *aa*·mi *buj*'·țe paar·ch'i na

BODO

Hopefully you won't find yourself *bunhan bunahan* (about to speak, and about not to speak at the same time) in the home of Bodo in India, Bodoland Territorial Areas District, in the northeastern state of Assam, but will rather be engaging with the local. It's true that there is a saying in Bodo that 'a deer dies due to its footstep; a man dies due to his mouth'. But try to work up some courage and don't be *gabkhron* (afraid of witnessing an adventure)!

The Bodo tribal people, sometimes called the Mech, fought long and hard for their language as well as the autonomy of their district, so learning a few words is bound to be appreciated. Bodo (pronounced *bo·ro*) was finally granted official status in India in 2003. As you might expect, given that Bodoland is wedged up against the Bhutan border, the language is part of the rich group of Tibeto-Burman languages, along with Burmese, Tibetan and Dzongka, the language of Bhutan.

Despite taking written form little more than one century ago, Bodo's community of 1.4 million speakers have one of the most vibrant, up-and-coming literary cultures in India. With much of its poetry, novels and stories drawing on its wealth of folklore and proverbs, Bodo can truly be said to *khen* (hit one's heart).

DOGRI

There are mentions of the Dogri language from the 13th century onwards, although the earliest written example is from the 18th century.

For much of its life, though, the Dogri language suffered an identity crisis – it was considered a dialect of Punjabi. True, both languages belong to the Indo-Aryan language family, and both use tones (that is, a word's meaning can depend on whether your voice falls or rises in pitch). But in 1969 Dogri was recognised as a language in its own right by a panel of official linguists.

Originally written in the ancient Takri script, Dogri has more recently adopted the Devanagari script.

Some say that the name of the Dogri-speaking region in the northern state of Jammu and Kashmir, Duggar, comes from the word 'invincible'; others say it's derived from a word that means, a bit more mundanely, 'hill'.

Dogri's some 2.3 million speakers certainly have a history of being *kacha* (tough) – look up the Dogra Regiment and Jammu and Kashmir Rifles to find out more! Better yet, try asking a Dogra (Dogri speaker) *Das keeyaan* (Tell me how it happened) to get the inside story.

GUJARATI

Gujarati (ગુજરાતી gu·ja·raa·tee), spoken by approximately 46 million people in India (primarily in the state of Gujarat) was the mother tongue of Mohandas Karamchand Gandhi. 'Gandhi' means 'grocer' in Gujarati, although the great Mahatma was certainly not restricted in life by his apparent ancestral profession. Gandhi, thought of as the father of the modern Indian nation, was also referred to as બાપુ baa·pu (lit: father) throughout India. He was passionate about his native language and wrote a number of works in Gujarati, many of which were later translated into English. Gujarati has a rich literary tradition and is written in the Gujarati script.

Like most other languages of northern India, Gujarati is a member of the Indo-Aryan language family. Gujarati has been further influenced by literary Sanskrit, Farsi and, more recently, Portuguese and English. The English words 'bungalow' and 'tank' both have their origins in Gujarati, from બંગલો bang·a·lo and ટાંકુ tan·kung respectively.

Have a crack at the language of the champion of nonviolence – should you make mistakes, there's certainly nothing to fear from its generous speakers!

The following are a few essentials in Gujarati:

Yes./No.	હા./ના.	haa/naa
Please.	પ્લીઝ.	pleez
Hello.	નમસ્તે.	na·mas·te/
Goodbye.	આવજો.	aav·jo
Thank you.	આભાર.	aa·b'aar
Excuse me. (to get past)	જરા જવા દેશો.	ja·raa ja·vaa de·sho
Excuse me. (to get attention)	એકસક્યુઝ મી.	eks·kyuz mi
Sorry.	માફ કરજો.	maap' kar·jo
Do you speak English?		
તમે ઇંગ્લીશ બોલો છો?		ta·me ang·re·jee bo·lo ch'o
I (don't) understand.		
સમજાયું (નહી).		sam·jaa·yung (na·heeng)

HINDI

Hindi (हिन्दी *hin·*dee) belongs to the Indo-Aryan group of the Indo-European language family. It has about 180 million native speakers in India. Hindi languages appeared in the Indus Valley at about the start of the Common Era, and by the European Middle Ages became known as 'Hindvi'. During the Islamic Mughal Empire, which ruled northern India from the 16th century until it was defeated by the British Raj in the mid-19th century, the Hindi-speaking Hindu population adopted many new words from Arabic, Farsi and Turkish but continued to write in Devanagari script, while the version written in Arabic script became known as Urdu. However, Hindi and Urdu share a common core vocabulary and are generally considered to be one spoken language, called Hindustani, which is written with two different scripts.

After Britain gave up its rule and Partition in 1947, Hindi was granted official status along with English, with 21 other languages recognised in the Constitution. The contact between the two languages is reflected in their vocabulary – 'jungle', 'khaki', 'pyjama', 'shampoo' and 'veranda' are just some of the common words that entered English from Hindi.

The following are a few essentials in Hindi:

Hello.	नमस्ते ।	na·ma·*ste*
Goodbye.	नमस्ते ।	na·ma·*ste*
Please ...	कृपया	kri·pa·*yaa* ...
Thank you.	शैबक्यू ।	*thaynk·*yoo
Yes.	जी हाँ ।	jee haang
No.	जी नहीं ।	jee na·*heeng*
Excuse me.	सुनिये ।	su·ni·ye
Sorry.	माफ़ कीजिये ।	maaf *kee·*ji·ye
Help!	मदद कीजिये!	ma·*dad kee·*ji·ye

Do you speak (English)?

| क्या आपको (अंग्रेज़ी) | kyaa aap ko (an·*gre·*zee) |
| आती है? | *aa·*tee hay |

I don't understand.

| मैं नहीं | mayng na·*heeng* |
| समझा/समझी । | *sam·*jaa/*sam·*jee m/f |

KANNADA

Fancy being able to impress former Miss World and darling of Bollywood, Aishwarya Rai, in her native tongue? Try some Kannada phrases, such as: ನೀವು ಬಹಳ ಸುಂದರವಾಗಿದೀರ! (nee·vu ba·ha·ḷa sun·da·ra·vaa·gi·dee·ra) 'You are very beautiful!'.

Native speakers of Kannada (ಕನ್ನಡ kan·na·da), like Ms Rai, are called Kannadigas (ಕನ್ನಡಿಗರು kan·na·di·ga·ru) and there are approximately 38 million of them in India, mostly located in the southern Indian state of Karnataka, as well as in some neighbouring states.

A Dravidian language related to Tamil and Malayalam, Kannada is written in its own distinct script. It has a long written tradition – recent archaeological finds of copper-plate inscriptions of the Ganga kings of Talakadu give evidence of written Kannada dating back at least 1500 years.

There are several different dialects of Kannada and, in the past, the dialect someone spoke could generally be predicted according to caste (determined by structure of Hindu society), although class (determined by wealth and education) is becoming a more important indicator in modern times. The literary and everyday spoken versions of Kannada also differ considerably.

With the few essential phrases provided here – you'll be ready to talk to the people at the local market, as well as Bollywood celebrities!

Yes./No.	ಹೌದು./ಇಲ್ಲ.	how·ḍu/il·la
Please.	ದಯವಿಟ್ಟು.	ḍa·ya·vit·tu
Hello./Goodbye.	ನಮಸ್ಕಾರ./	na·mas·kaa·ra/
	ಸಿಗೋಣ.	si·goh·ṇa
Thank you.	ಥ್ಯಾಂಕ್ಯೂ.	t'ank·yoo
Excuse me. (to get past)	ಸ್ವಲ್ಪ ದಾರಿ ಬಿಡಿ.	sval·pa ḍaa·ri bi·di
Sorry.	ಕ್ಷಮಿಸಿ.	ksha·mi·si

Do you speak English?

ನೀವು ಇಂಗ್ಲೀಷ್	nee·vu ing·*lee*·shu
ಮಾತಾಡುತ್ತೀರ?	maa·taa·duṭ·ṭee·ra

I don't understand.

ನನಗೆ ಅರ್ಥವಾಗುವುದಿಲ್ಲ.	na·na·ge ar·ṭ'a·aa·gu·vu·dil·la

KASHMIRI

We can thank the Kashmiri, experts in cheating the Himalayan chill, for the word 'cashmere' in English. Kashmiri (कश्मीरी kash·mee·ree) is spoken in the valley of Kashmir at the foothills of the Himalayas: a beautiful area, situated mostly in the Jammu and Kashmir state of India. There are around 5.5 million speakers of Kashmiri, which is a member of the Dardic subgroup of the Indo-Aryan language family. It's written using a variation of the Perso-Arabic script or, as below, in the Devanagari script.

You might try impressing the locals with your knowledge of some of their colourful proverbs such as ॲकिस दज़ान दॅर ब्याख् वुं शनावान अथ' (eu·kis da·zaan deūr byaak' vush·naa·vaan at') 'When one man's beard is on fire, another man warms his hands on it' meaning 'People often take advantage of someone else's misery'.

The following are a few essentials in Kashimiri:

Yes./No.	आ ‍‍। न ‍‍।	aa/na
Please.	मेहरबॉनी ‍‍।	me·har·beū·nee
Hello./Goodbye.	आदाब ‍‍।/अलविदा ‍‍।	aa·daab/al·vi·daa
Thank you.	शुक्रिया ‍‍।	shuk·ri·yaa
Excuse me. (to get past)	वथ त्रॉविव ‍‍।	vat' treū·viv
Excuse me. (to get attention)	यपॉर्य ‍‍।	ya·peūry
Sorry.	माफ कॅरिव ‍‍।	maap' keu·riv

Do you speak English?
तोह्य छिवा अंगरीज़ी बोलान?   tohy ch'i·vaa ang·ree·zee bo·laan

I (don't) understand.
ब' छुस/छस (न') ज़ानान ‍‍।   biu ch'us/ch'as (niu) zaa·naan m/f

KONKANI

The approximately 2.5 million Konkani speakers living in India are a diverse lot: they live on the west coast of India in the states of Goa, Karnataka, Maharashtra, Gujarat and Kerala; they practise Hinduism, Christianity and Islam; and they write their language in the Devanagari, Roman, Arabic, Kannada and Malayalam scripts. In 1987, after years of political debate, Konkani (ಕೊಂಕ್ಣಿ *konk·nee*) finally became the official language of Goa – the home of trance music and Goan prawn curry, and once a colony of Portugal.

The name Goa is reportedly derived from the Konkani word ಗೊಂಯಾಂ *go·yan* (meaning 'a patch of tall grass') though Goa is probably better known for its beautiful beaches. An Indo-Aryan language related to Gujarati and Marathi, Konkani has also been influenced over the years by Sanskrit, Portuguese, Perso-Arabic and Kannada. The Devanagari script (used to write Hindi and Marathi) is now the official writing system for Konkani in Goa. However, a large number of Konkani speakers in Karnataka write Konkani in the Kannada script, as used in this chapter. So don't get stuck in a Goan trance – get out there and have a go at speaking Konkani!

The following are a few essentials in Konkani:

Yes./No.	ವ್ಯಯ್./ನಾಂ.	*weu·*i/naang
Please.	ಉಪ್ಕಾರ್ ಕರ್ನ್	*up·*kaar keürn
Hello./Goodbye.	ಹಲ್ಲೋ./ಮೆಳ್ಯಾಂ.	*hal·*lo/*mej·*yaang
Thank you.	ದೇವ್ ಬರೆಂ ಕರುಂ.	*ɖay·*u bo·reng ko·roong
Excuse me. (to get past)	ಮ್ಯಾಕಾ ವಚೊಂಕ್ ಸೊಡ್.	m'aa·kaa wo·ts'onk ts'od
Excuse me. (to get attention)	ಉಪ್ಕಾರ್ ಕರ್ನ್	*up·*kaar keürn
Sorry.	ಚೂಕ್ ಝಾಲಿ, ಮಾಫ್ ಕರ್.	ts'ook *zaa·*li maaf keür

Do you speak English?
ಇಂಗ್ಲಿಶ್ ಉಲೆಯ್ತಾಯ್ಗೀ?   *ing·*leesh *u·*leuy·ţaay·gee
I don't understand.
ನಾಂ, ಸಮ್ಝೊಕ್–ನಾಂ.   naang *som·*zonk·naang

MAITHILI

While you're likely to find plain phrases like *Kail ke yatra kaina rahal?* (How was the journey yesterday?) or *Aahan ke naam kee chee?* (What's your name?), the most useful when chatting to speakers of Maithili, the language's history is really quite romantic. Its rise is credited to the 14th-century poet Vidyapati, a trailblazer comparable to Chaucer in England or Dante in Italy. It's said that the beauty of his Maithili poetry influenced the king of the time to begin using the language for official purposes instead of Sanskrit.

Maithili has had a fertile literary tradition from that time right up to the present day. Nevertheless, like some other Indo-Aryan languages, for a long period Maithili was considered to be a variety of Hindi, and it only became an official language in 2004.

These days, Maithili is spoken by some 22 million people in India, mainly in the state of Bihar in the northeast, and by around 2.8 million more people in Nepal. In keeping with its educated status, it tends to be associated with Brahmin and high-caste Hindus, so it pays to brush up on your Maithili pleasantries.

Yes./No.	हँ/नय ।	ha-n/na-e
Please.	कृपया ।	kri-pa-ya
Hello.	नमस्कार ।	na-mas-kaar
Hello. (with respect)	प्रणाम ।	pra-naam
Goodbye.	नमस्कार ।	na-mas-kaar
Goodbye. (with respect)	प्रणाम ।	pra-naam
Thank you.	धन्यबाद ।	dhan-ya-baad
Excuse me.	सुनु त ।	su-nu ta
Sorry.	क्षमा करू ।	ksha-ma ka-ru

Do you speak (English)?

कि अहाँ (अँग्रेजी) बाजै छी ?   ki a-ha (ang-re-gi) ba-jai chi

I don't understand.

हम नय बुझली ।   hum na-e bhuj-lau

MALAYALAM

Malayalam (മലയാളം ma·la·ya·*lam*) is a Dravidian language related to Tamil, in which its name is purported to mean 'language of the mountain region'. It has approximately 33 million speakers, primarily in the Indian state of Kerala – self-proclaimed to be 'God's own country', known around the world for its pristine natural beauty. Malayalam is written in the wonderfully curly Malayalam script, used in this chapter, and occasionally also in the Arabic script.

This language is the source of the English words 'copra' (dried coconut), from the Malayalam കൊപ്പര (kop·*pa*·ra), and 'teak' (brown colour), from the Malayalam തേക്ക് (tek·*ka*). Other culturally significant Malayalam terms include *mundu* (മുണ്ടു mun·*tu*), the local white- or cream-coloured version of the ubiquitous Indian dhoti, and *Kalarippayatt* (കളരിപ്പയറ്റ് ka·la·*rip*·pa·jat·*t'i*), a local form of martial arts. A huge 40% of the Malayalam vocabulary can be traced back to borrowings from Sanskrit.

The language is, however, rapidly moving into modern times, with influence from English as well as the coining of new terms, such as *adipoli* (അടിപൊളി a·*di*·po·li) which is equivalent to 'awesome' or 'wow' in English and is used by young Malayalis. So give the following words and phrases a try – they're totally, like, *adipoli*!

Yes./No.	അതെ./അല്ല.	a·*t'e*/al·la
Please.	ദയവായി.	da·ya·va·yi
Hello./Goodbye.	ഹലോ./ഗുഡ് ബൈ.	ha·*lo*/good bai
Thank you.	നന്ദി.	nan·*n'i*
Excuse me. (to get past)	ക്ഷമിക്കണം.	ksha·mi·ka·*nam*
Excuse me. (to get attention)	ക്ഷമിക്കണം.	ksha·mi·ka·*nam*
Sorry.	ക്ഷമിക്കുക.	ksha·mi·ku·*ka*

Do you speak English?
നിങ്ങൾ ഇംഗ്ലീഷ് സംസാരിക്കുമോ?   ning·*al* in·*glish* şam·*saa*·ri·ku·*mo*

I don't understand.
എനിക്ക് മനസ്സിലാകില്ല.   e·ni·*ku* ma·na·şi·la·ki·la

MANIPURI

The official language of the Himalayan state of Manipur, Manipuri has quite a few other names: among them 'Meitei', 'Meiteilon', 'Meiteilol', 'Meithei' and 'Pangal-lol'. Confusingly, there's also an Indo-Aryan language spoken in Manipur called Bishnupriya Manipuri, with some 450,000 speakers. 'Manipuri' is perhaps its loveliest name, though, translating as 'the language of the land of the jewel'.

Manipuri is the language of the Meitei people of Manipur – described as 'the Switzerland of India' due to its beautiful mountains and valleys and mild climate. A Tibeto-Burman language, Manipuri is also spoken in nearby states such as Assam, Tripura and Nagaland and the neighbouring countries of Bangladesh and Myanmar, with around 1.25 million speakers all up. And while it's written in the Bengali script, efforts have been made since the 1940s to revive and reconstruct the ancient Manipuri script – and why not? It's as graceful as the Manipuru form of classical dance, popularised throughout India in the 1920s by poet and composer Rabindranath Tagore.

MARATHI

Bollywood fans may already recognise some of the more colourful Marathi expressions. Mumbai slang (मुंबईचा mum·bai·cha), a rough-and-ready mix of Hindi, Marathi, Gujarati, Konkani and English, has become a regular feature in the popular Hindi films, taking Marathi to cinemas all over the world.

Spoken by an estimated 71 million people, Marathi (मराठी ma·raa·t'i) is the official language in Maharashtra and is also spoken in bordering areas. Perhaps even more important to know, at least when talking to some of India's mad cricket fans, it's the language of cricketing icon and Mumbai native Sachin Tendulkar.

Marathi belongs to the southern branch of the Indo-Aryan language family, although it additionally bears the influence of neighbouring languages Telugu and Kannada. Turkish, Arabic, Portuguese and Farsi have also left their mark – many words from these languages have become part of the Marathi lexicon.

Present-day written Marathi is a slightly modified version of the Devanagari script (used for Hindi) and is encouragingly called बाळबोध (bal·bod), meaning 'can be understood by a child'. While you don't need to master the writing to communicate with the मुंबईकर (mum·bai·kar) 'people of Mumbai', the phrases below will certainly help you on your way.

Yes./No.	होय./नाही.	hoy/naa·hee
Please.	कृपया.	kri·pa·yaa
Hello./Goodbye.	नमस्कार../बाय.	na·mas·kaar/bai
Thank you.	धन्यवाद.	d'an·ya·vaad
Excuse me. (to get past)	जरा जाऊ देता.	ja·raa jaa·oo de·ṭaa
Excuse me. (to get attention)	क्षमस्व	ksha·mas·va
Sorry.	खेद आहे.	k'eḍ aa·he

Do you speak English?
आपण इंग्रजी बोलता का ?   aa·paṇ ing·re·jee bol·ṭaa kaa
I (don't) understand.
मला समजत (नाही).   ma·laa sam·jaṭ (naa·hee)

Official languages of India

NEPALI

Kaṭhmahḍaū jahne bahṭo dherai lahmo cha 'It's a long way to Kathmandu'. You probably know that Nepali is the national language in Nepal – it's spoken by 11 million people there and acts as an important unifying force, given there are no fewer than 100 indigenous languages. What many people don't know is that Nepali, the mountain language (Parbatiya), is also an official language in India. It has 6 million speakers there, mostly in the northeastern areas close to Nepal like Darjeeling, Sikkim and Assam. (There are also a scattering of around 150,000 Nepali speakers in Bhutan.)

Another interesting fact is that Nepali is closely related to Hindi, and Nepali and Hindi speakers can often understand one another; both languages belong to the Indo-Aryan language family.

For language learners, the great thing about Nepali is that, like many other languages around the world, including English, words often do double or triple duty for you. For instance, *rahmro* means 'good', but can also mean 'nice' or 'beautiful', depending on the context. And the classic example is *namaste* – 'hello', 'goodbye' and 'best wishes' all in one word!

The following are a few essentials in Nepali:

Hello./Goodbye.	नमस्ते	na·ma·*ste*
Hello./Goodbye.	नमस्कार	na·ma·*skahr* (pol)
I'm sorry	माफ गर्नंहोस	mahph *gar*·nu·hos
Excuse me, sir/madam. (to get attention)	यो दाइ/दिदी	yo, dai/*di*·di
Do you speak English?		
तपाई अङ्ग्रेजी	ta·*paī* ang·*gre*·ji	
भाषा बोल्नुहन्छ ?	*bhah*·sah *bol*·nu·hun·cha?	
I don't understand.		
मैले बझीन	*mai*·le bu·*jhi*·na	

Yes./No. These words are said in several ways in Nepali. For more information see the Lonely Planet Nepali Phrasebook.

ORIYA

The great Jagannatha temple at Puri in Orissa houses some of the earliest Oriya writing, contained in the 12th-century *Madala Panji* (Palm-leaf Chronicles). Now spoken by approximately 31 million people, Oriya (ଓଡ଼ିଆ o·di·aa) is the state language of Orissa, and has speakers in West Bengal and Gujarat.

Historically very similar to Bengali, Oriya is believed to have come into its own in the 10th and 11th centuries. It was during this period that politics brought the western and coastal dialects of the Orissa region together, and a common language evolved. It went on to develop a rich literary tradition, with many writers mastering the art of poetry in particular. The modern state of Orissa wasn't declared until after Indian independence in 1947, when the Oriya-speaking peoples were finally united.

Oriya belongs to the eastern group of the Indo-Aryan language family and, in addition to Bengali, it has a close relative in Assamese. Despite these connections, the Oriya speakers preferred a different writing system to that of other languages of the same family, and adopted a script that employs fewer straight lines.

The following are a few essentials in Oriya:

Yes./No.	ହଁ./ନା.	han/naa
Please.	ଦୟାକରୀ.	da·yaa·ka·ri
Hello./Goodbye.	ଆଦ୍ଦେ./ବିଦାୟ.	aa·he/bi·da·ya
Thank you.	ଧନ୍ୟବାଦ.	d'an·ya·baa·da
Excuse me. (to get past)	କ୍ଷମା କରିବେ.	k'ya·maa ka·ri·be
Excuse me. (to get attention)	କ୍ଷମା କରନ୍ତୁ.	k'ya·maa ka·ran·tu
Sorry.	ଦୁଃଖିତ.	du·k'i·ta

Do you speak English?
ଆପଣ ଇଂରାଜୀ କହୁନ୍ତି କି?   aa·pa·n'a eng·li·sha ku·han·ti ki
I (don't) understand.
ମୁଁ ବୁଝେ (ନାହିଁ).   mu bu·j'e (naa·hi)

PUNJABI

You may not speak it yet, but with an estimated 60 million Punjabi speakers worldwide chances are you've heard it. If you've seen the film *Bend it like Beckham*, or enjoyed the rhythms of **bhangra** music, then you've already had a taste of this lively language.

Part of the Indo-Aryan language family and related to Hindi and Urdu, Punjabi (ਪੰਜਾਬੀ *pan·jaa·bee*) is spoken by more than 27 million people in India. While it's the official language of the state of Punjab, it's also spoken in the Punjab region of Pakistan and in Bangladesh. Thanks to a long-running diaspora, large communities of Punjabi speakers are also found in far-flung places such as Kenya, Singapore, Fiji, Malaysia, the UK, Canada and the US. The Gurmukhi script – meaning 'from the mouth of the guru' – is Punjabi's chief written medium in India (whereas Shahmukhi script is used in Pakistan) and was standardised by the Sikh Guru Angad in the 16th century. The alphabet is phonetic, which means that every letter generally corresponds to one sound. But be prepared: like most Indian languages, Punjabi is not for the lazy-tongued – so get your mouth and lungs warmed up and start mixing with the locals.

The following are a few essentials in Punjabi:

Yes./No.	ਹਾਂ/ ਨਹੀਂ।	haang/ neyng
Please.	ਕਿਰਪਾ ਕਰਕੇ।	*kir*·pa kar·*key*
Hello./Goodbye.	ਸਤਿ ਸ੍ਰੀ ਅਕਾਲ।	sat sree a·*kaal*
Thank you.	ਧੰਨਵਾਦ।	d'an·waad
Excuse me. (to get past)	ਧਿਆਨ ਦੇਣਾ।	d'i·*aan* dey·*naa*
Excuse me. (to get attention)	ਧਿਆਨ ਦੇਣਾ।	d'i·*aan* dey·*naa*
Sorry.	ਮਾਫ ਕਰਨਾ।	maaf *kar*·naa

Do you speak English?
ਕੀ ਤੁਸੀਂ ਅੰਗਰੇਜੀ
ਬੋਲਦੇ ਹੋ?
kee tu·*seeng* an·*grey*·jee bol·*dey* ho

I (don't) understand.
ਮੈਂ (ਨਹੀਂ) ਸਮਝਿਆ।
maeng (neyng) sa·mij'·ya

SANSKRIT

Two thousand years ago, India was arguably the spiritual and intellectual hotspot of the world, and Sanskrit was the langauge of choice of its scholars. As a result Sanskrit became a classical language of India, much like Latin and Ancient Greek are in Europe.

Sanskrit no longer has any real native speakers, but, like Latin and Ancient Greek, it is still studied. In addition, it remains an important langauge of religion and a number of people in India know it as a second language, used mainly for Hindu hymns and mantras.

Many important ancient texts were written in Sanskrit: the beloved Hindu epics *Ramayana* and *Mahabharata* (see box p70), and Pāṇini's grammar of Sanskrit, which is one of the oldest in the world and which has a continuing influence on modern grammarians.

In addition to Pāṇini's famous grammar, Sankrit has further influenced modern scholarship through its very existence. In the 18th century, Enlightenment scholar Sir William Jones famously (and, at the time, quite controversally) noted the similarity of Sanskrit to Latin and Ancient Greek. As he predicted, this similarity was no coincidence, and it was later demonstrated that Sanskrit, along with Hindi and many other languages of India, is a member of the Indo-Aryan language subfamily of the larger Indo-European language family. This means that Sankrit is related to English and many other languages of Europe (see box p11).

SANTHALI

Among the many passionate linguists of India, Pandit Raghunath Murmu, popularly known as 'Guru Gomke', stands out. In the early 20th century, he felt that his native tongue Santhali was being stuffed into the Devanagari, Bengali and Roman alphabets like feet into ill-fitting shoes, and that it was holding the language back. So, Murmu set about inventing his own script, Ol Chiki ('writing learning'), making use of symbols familar to Santhali speakers. (Unlike most of the languages in northeast India, which tend to belong to the Indo-Aryan or Tibeto-Burman language families, Santhali is an Austro-Asiatic language like Khmer and Vietnamese.) Ol Chiki was launched to the public in 1925. Many books and magazines have been published in it, but sadly, the literacy rate in Santhali – whether in Ol Chiki or any other script – remains at around 10% to 30% of all speakers. The language is spoken by around 6.5 million people in the northeastern states of India, including Assam, Bihar, Orissa and Tripura, plus small numbers in Bangladesh, Bhutan and Nepal.

SINDHI

Sindhi, the Indo-Aryan language of the tribal people of the same name, doesn't do anything by halves. Not only does it use a huge range of sounds (no fewer than 46 consonants and 16 vowels), it has a giant vocabulary and a wealth of poetry and literature – how could it not, with 4000 years of culture behind it? Evidence for this are the remains of the ancient Indus Valley civilization located in Sindh province in Pakistan called Mohenjo-daro, which means 'mound of the dead' in Sindhi. Although it is not known what the language of this ancient civilization was, there is at least some connection with Sindh culture as the famous 'Priest King' sculpture found there is wearing a Sindh *ajruk* 'shawl'.

While the bulk of Sindhi's speakers (18.5 million) still live across the border in Pakistan's Sindh Province, it's also an official language in India and has nearly 3 million speakers there, as well as some overseas. The speakers of Sindhi in India are mostly Hindus who fled Pakistan after the Partition and are now scattered throughout various states of India, with the majority residing in Maharashtra and Gujarat.

Sindhi is also a fund of proverbs, including drily humorous gems like *Jeda utha, teda loda* (The bigger the camel, the bigger the jerks it experiences).

Want to get to know the locals? The following phrases will stand you in good stead:

Yes.	हा	haa
No.	नह	nah
Please.	मेहरबानी करे	me·har·baa·nee ka·ray
Hello.	कीयाँ आहियो?	kee·yang aa·hi·yo
Goodbye.	वरी मिलन्दों सीं	va·ree mi·lan·daang seeng
Thank you.	मेहरबानी	me·har·baa·nee
Sorry.	माफ करियो	maaf ka·ri·yo

TAMIL

Ever wondered who made the first curry? While experts may dispute the origins of the dish, it's almost certain that the Tamil word கறி (*ka·ri*) gave us its English name. With records of the language's existence going back more than 2000 years, it's not surprising that many Tamil words have been shared around. English also owes Tamil thanks for மிளகு தண்ணீ (mi·la·*ku* tan·*ni*) 'pepper water', known to many as 'mulligatawny', and for கட்டு மரம் (kat·*tu* ma·*ram*) 'tied logs', from which 'catamaran' is derived.

Spoken by about 62 million people in India, Tamil (தமிழ் *ta·mil*) is the official language of the Indian state Tamil Nadu, as well as a national language in Sri Lanka, Malaysia and Singapore. Tamil belongs to the Tamil-Kannada group from the southern branch of the Dravidian language family. It was confirmed a 'classical language' of India in 2004 – one of only two languages with this status (Sanskrit is the other). The Tamil script is aptly named வட்டெழுத்து (vat·*te*·lut·tu) 'rounded writing' – so styled because curved lines were gentler on palm leaves, the traditional material for writing.

The following are a few essentials in Tamil:

Yes./No.	ஆமாம்./இல்லை.	*aa*·maam/*il*·lai
Please.	தயவு செய்து.	ta·ya·*vu* chey·*tu*
Hello.	வணக்கம்.	va·*nak*·kam
Goodbye.	போய் வருகிறேன்.	*po*·i va·*ru*·ki·ren
Thank you.	நன்றி.	*nan*·dri
Excuse me.	கொளுஞ்சம்	*kony*·nyam
(to get past)	நகருங்கள்.	na·*ka*·rung·kaḷ
Excuse me.	தயவு செய்து.	ta·ya·*vu* sei·*du*
(to get attention)		
Sorry.	மன்னிக்கவும.	*man*·nik·ka·vum

Do you speak English?

நீங்கள் ஆங்கிலம்   *neeng*·kaḷ *aang*·ki·lam
பேசுவீர்களா?   *pey*·chu·*veer*·ka·ḷa

I don't understand.

எனக்கு   e·*nak*·ku
வீளங்கவில்லை.   vi·*lang*·ka·vil·*ley*

TELUGU

There are many theories about the origins of the name 'Telugu' (also known as Tenugu), but perhaps the most endearing one is that it's derived from the word తేన (te·ne) 'honey', thus making Telugu (తెలుగు te·lu·gu) 'the language of honey'.

The official home of this south-central Dravidian language is Andhra Pradesh, where it achieved official status in 1966. It's spoken by around 70 million people there, as well as in parts of Tamil Nadu. As with many Indian languages, migration has taken Telugu offshore and it's spoken in Malaysia, Singapore, Fiji, Mauritius and parts of the Middle East. The geography of its home state, which spreads into the heart of India, has allowed Telugu to be enriched over time by both Indo-Aryan and Dravidian languages.

Local poets first mused in the language in the 11th century, and it has long been associated with the classical Carnatic music. Telugu has four regional dialects – northern, southern, eastern and central – with central considered the standard.

A few honeyed Telugu phrases will go a long way whichever region you're in. The following few essentials in Telugu will help you to get started:

Yes./No.	అవును./కాదు.	a·vu·nu/kaa·du
Please.	దయచేసి.	da·ya·chay·si
Hello.	నమస్కారం.	na·mas·kaa·ram
Goodbye.	ఎళ్ళొస్తాను.	vel·loh·staa·nu
Thank you.	ధన్యవాదాలు.	d'an·ya·vaa·daa·lu
Excuse me.	కొంచెం పక్కకు	kohn·chem pak·ka·ku
(to get past)	జరగండి.	ja·ra·gan·di
Excuse me.	ఏమండి.	ay·an·di
(to get attention)		
Sorry.	క్షమించండి.	ksha·min·chan·di

Do you speak English?

మీరు ఇంగ్లీషు	mee·ru ing·lee·shu
మాట్లాడుతారా?	maat·laa·du·taa·raa

I don't understand.

అర్థం కాదు.	ar·t'am kaa·du

URDU

An Indo-Aryan language, Urdu (اردو *ur*·doo) has around 50 million speakers in India and is an official language in Bihar and Jammu, and Kashmir. Urdu and Hindi are generally considered to be one spoken language with two different scripts. When Muslim Turks invaded Punjab in 1027 and took control of Delhi in 1193, they paved the way for the Islamic Mughal Empire, which ruled northern India from the 16th century until the mid-19th century. It was during this time that the Muslim speakers of the language known as 'Hindvi' began to write in Arabic script. Another variation between Hindi and Urdu is that, despite their common ancestry, much of Urdu's academic and philosophical vocabulary is of Arabic or Farsi origin. In the years leading up to the partition of India and Pakistan in 1947, the question of language in Britain's India was strongly linked to religious and cultural pride. Urdu was seen as a Muslim-only language and was accordingly chosen as the national language of Pakistan.

The following are a few essentials in Urdu:

Yes.	جی ہاں۔	jee haang
No.	جی نہیں۔	jee na·*heeng*
Please ...	مہربانی	me·har·baa·nee
	کرکے ...	kar ke ...
Hello.	السلام عالیکم۔	as·sa·laam a·*lay*·kum
Goodbye.	خدا حافظ۔	ku·*daa* haa·fiz
Thank you.	شکریہ۔	*shuk*·ri·yah
Excuse me.	راستہ دے	*raas*·taa de
(to get past)	دیجیے۔	*dee*·ji·ye
Excuse me.	سنئے۔	su·ni·ye
(to get attention)		
Sorry.	معاف کیجیے۔	maaf *kee*·ji·ye

Do you speak (English)?

کیا آپ کو (انگریزی) آتی ہے؟

kyaa aap ko (an·*gre*·zee) aa·tee hay

No, I don't understand.

میں نہیں سمجھا/ سمجھی۔

mayng na·*heeng* sam·jaa/ sam·jee **m/f**

B

WORDFINDER

199

G

I

J

N

Y

Z

What kind of traveller are you?

A. You're eating chicken for dinner *again* because it's the only word you know.

B. When no one understands what you say, you step closer and shout louder.

C. When the barman doesn't understand your order, you point frantically at the beer.

D. You're surrounded by locals, swapping jokes, email addresses and experiences – other travellers want to borrow your phrasebook or audio guide.

If you answered A, B, or C, you NEED Lonely Planet's language products ...

- **Lonely Planet Phrasebooks** – for every phrase you need in every language you want
- **Lonely Planet Language & Culture** – get behind the scenes of English as it's spoken around the world – learn and laugh
- **Lonely Planet Fast Talk & Fast Talk Audio** – essential phrases for short trips and weekends away – read, listen and talk like a local
- **Lonely Planet Small Talk** – 10 essential languages for city breaks
- **Lonely Planet Real Talk** – downloadable language audio guides from lonelyplanet.com to your MP3 player

... and this is why

- **Talk to everyone everywhere**
  Over 120 languages, more than any other publisher
- **The right words at the right time**
  Quick-reference colour sections, two-way dictionary, easy pronunciation, every possible subject – and audio to support it

Lonely Planet Offices

Australia
90 Maribyrnong St, Footscray,
Victoria 3011
☎ 03 8379 8000
fax 03 8379 8111
✉ talk2us@lonelyplanet.com.au

USA
150 Linden St, Oakland,
CA 94607
☎ 510 250 6400
fax 510 893 8572
✉ info@lonelyplanet.com

UK
2nd floor, 186 City Rd
London EC1V 2NT
☎ 020 7106 2100
fax 020 7106 2101
✉ go@lonelyplanet.co.uk

lonelyplanet.com